SHARING THE VISION

THE CHURCH'S TEACHING SERIES

Prepared at the request of the Executive Council of the
General Convention of the Episcopal Church

SHARING
THE VISION

THE CHURCH'S TEACHING SERIES READER

Edited by Ruth Cheney
Contributions by Robert A. Bennett, John E. Booty,
Earl H. Brill, O. C. Edwards, Urban T. Holmes III,
Rachel Hosmer, Alan Jones, Richard A. Norris,
Charles P. Price, Louis Weil, and John H. Westerhoff III.

THE SEABURY PRESS / NEW YORK

1980
The Seabury Press
815 Second Avenue
New York, N. Y. 10017

Printed in the United States of America

Library of Congress Cataloging in Publication Data

Main entry under title:
Sharing the vision.

"Contains excerpts from the seven volumes of the Church's
teaching series."
1. Protestant Episcopal Church in the U.S.A.—Doctrinal and
controversial works—Addresses, essays, lectures. I. Bennett,
Robert A., 1933- II. Cheney, Ruth.
BX5935.S43   230'.3   79-27021
ISBN 0-8164-2044-0

Preface

This is a collection of readings from the new Church's Teaching Series. The volume contains excerpts from the seven volumes of the Church's Teaching Series—chosen because they speak to the reader with limited time. Each selection is preceded by an introduction that poses study questions. It is our sincere hope that the reader will be inquisitive and want to learn more. The project has been both challenging and exciting. Not only is there a wide variety of opinions regarding the substance of the teaching of the Church, there are also varying and conflicting views with regard to the methods of communicating this teaching to others. That is why we have tried to pay close attention to the various movements within the Church, and to address them. The development of this new series, therefore, has involved hundreds of men and women throughout the Episcopal Church and is offered as one resource among many for the purposes of Christian education.

While it is neither possible, nor perhaps even desirable today to produce a definitive series of books setting forth the specific teachings of a particular denomination, we have tried to emphasize the element of continuity between this new series and the old. Continuity, however, implies movement, and we believe that the new series breaks fresh ground in a creative and positive way.

The new series makes modest claims. It speaks not so much *for* the Episcopal Church as *to* it, and not to this Church only but to Christians of other traditions, and to those who wait expectantly at the edge of the Church.

Two words have been in constant use to describe this project from its inception: affirmation and exploration. The writers have affirmed the great insights of the Christian tradition and have also explored new possibilities for the future in the confidence that the future is God's.

Alan Jones
CHAIRMAN OF THE
CHURCH'S TEACHING SERIES
COMMITTEE

INTRODUCTION

The seven volumes of the new Church's Teaching Series are special and unusual books. They came into being out of the creativity of a great many people. Their preparation and publication were requested by the General Convention and the Executive Council of the Episcopal Church; and in the process of their development the series reached far beyond the list of persons named in the front of each volume. Seen as a whole, across the spectrum of their subject areas, they are the expression of a vision of what it means, at this time in our history, in this Church, to be religious persons, thinking about God and humanity in disciplined ways, seeking to understand the nature and the resources of our faith.

The seven books are windows on our believing as Christians; on the Bible as a living force and as a channel for what God reveals through its words. We are helped to examine our participation in the Church through a sense of history which connects our present and our future with our past. *Liturgy for Living* is a rich exploration of our worship and how we live it. *Understanding the Faith of the Church* takes us on a search for the meaning of the nature of God, and moves us to the hard questions of our humanity and our difficulties with knowing and belief. *The Christian Moral Vision* is an honest book which evokes honesty in response, raising the moral and ethical issues of our daily lives and the broad moral and ethical issues of our society. *Living in the Spirit* is a refreshing affirmation of our spirituality as inborn and inevitable, helping us to see prayer as a gift and as a movement toward wholeness in Christ.

The title, *Sharing the Vision,* was chosen for this book because we hope and believe that the book will enable what its name suggests. It brings together carefully chosen portions of each volume of the Church's Teaching Series, connecting the selections with questions for thought and study and setting each selection in the context of the book from which it came.

Sharing the Vision makes it possible to appreciate the diversity and the richness of the entire series. We commend it as a valuable personal and group resource, complete in what it presents; but its principal purpose is to stimulate thought and to build bridges for its readers into the other volumes of the Church's Teaching Series.

Ruth Gordon Cheney
GENERAL EDITOR OF THE
CHURCH'S TEACHING SERIES

Contents

· 1 ·

Christian Believing

- Are you a religious person?
- If you answered "yes" to the first question, how do you *know* that you are religious?
- If you answered "no" to the first question, how do you *know* you're *not* religious? Is it that you do not regularly attend a church?
- Can you identify the turning points in your life? What changed as a result of them—can you remember?

Christian Believing is the first and most basic volume in The Church's Teaching Series. It was written well into the last quarter of the twentieth century. Many of our grandparents and great-grandparents would have been astounded at the idea that their descendants were reading this book. In their day, it was generally assumed, except in the most avant-garde circles, that one *did* believe in God and in some manifestation of his church on earth. In the past there certainly was diversity in doctrine and practice of religion—but there was no doubt of the absolute necessity of religion. But in the last quarter of the twentieth century, nothing can be, nor is, taken for granted. And perhaps that is all for the best.

This volume does not presume to tell the reader what he or she should believe. It performs a more valuable service for contemporary people. It helps them identify what they are already thinking and feeling. We have moved a long way from our grandparents' or great-grandparents' quick response on being asked about their beliefs—"Of course I believe in God";

1

"*Certainly* I'm a Christian!" We are, even the most sincere believers among us, so conditioned to living in a society perceived to be thoroughly and completely secular that we must examine and re-examine our beliefs in order to understand them.

The authors of *Christian Believing* lead the reader from an understanding of the basic need, the "hunger" for religion, as the authors put it, through an analysis of the different ways of believing, to an ultimate discussion of the ways in which belief is or can be acted out and acted upon in the contemporary world.

"Not by Bread Alone," the selection from *Christian Believing* which follows, is the bedrock discussion, the chapter that the authors use to help us understand how to identify the place in our lives that must be filled. This selection will at least begin to answer the questions that opened this discussion—and others as well.

Not by Bread Alone

We live in a society which makes every possible effort to assure us that religion is unnecessary. Perhaps this explains why for more than a century social scientists have predicted the end of religion. Still, no empirical evidence for the decline of religion exists; particular religious communities may come and go but the alleged demise of religion is simply unfounded. Indeed, we appear to be on the brink of a religious revival. Religion in one form or another is an abiding human phenomenon. There appear to be basic longings of the human spirit which nothing else can satisfy and which no human effort can finally suppress: humans cannot live by bread alone. Human life requires some sort of religion for survival.

When we use the word religion we are not talking about what *you* believe as compared to what *we* believe: Protestantism vs. Catholicism, Christianity vs. Hinduism. We are speaking of a motivating force similar to hunger. Humans, it appears, are by nature religious beings; they have an innate longing for cosmos, or order, in life's chaos.

Americans live in the presence of a great historic irony. Never have a people known a greater degree of economic security, social mobility, and educational opportunity; never have they had as great a potential for living long, healthy lives. At the same time, never a day passes that we are not in some way confronted by a gloomy depiction of the human condition. Few thinking people would be particularly surprised to learn that recently a group of high school students, when asked to write their first English papers, chose to write on the theme of their individual discovery of the precariousness of existence, their awareness that life can be cut off at any moment without warning, and their simultaneous discovery that the grown-up world (father and mother) cannot make everything all right.

Chaos appears to be an ever present human experience—but an experience most humans cannot bear. Humans innately respond to the threat of chaos by a thrust toward cosmos—that ideal of order where everything is arranged in proper relationship to everything else and the whole appears to be good, beautiful, and true. Humans are essentially religious because they possess a need for order, a need to make sense out of their lived experience, and a need to find answers to those questions most people eventually ask: Is there meaning to life in general and to my life in particular? What is my purpose? Does anybody care what happens to me?

The desire to moor our lives to some sort of ultimate meaning is as natural as eating. Ingmar Bergman, the Swedish film-maker, was quoted as saying, in effect, that "life without God is unbearable." Bergman, in this case, was neither affirming nor promoting a belief in the existence of God; he was suggesting that humans cannot live productively without some sense of an overarching meaning for life.

As the French philosopher Maurice Merleau-Ponty wrote, "Because we are present to the world, we are condemned to meaning." No matter how meaningless life may seem to be, as long as we live our humanity tells us that life must have meaning. That is why we are haunted and driven until we can discover this meaning and live accordingly.

The secret of the human life is not so much to live, as to live *for* something. Albert Camus, the French playwright and novelist, has suggested that it does not, after all, matter very much whether the earth goes round the sun or the sun goes round the earth—the only really serious question is whether, either way, our life is or is not worth living. In Paris in 1968, a time of student unrest, these words were painted on the walls of the University of Paris, *"survivre n'est pas vivre"* (survival isn't living). There simply has to be more to life than the vicissitudes of daily existence. To live is to search for ultimate meaning.

Religion, then, is best understood as both the quest for and the response to that which is truly ultimate. By ultimate we mean that which is fundamental to life, that which transcends the superficial world of provable fact, that which leads to some sense of a total experience in which we find a resolution for our lives, a sense of order, a mooring, and a meaning. As such, religion is more than a concern for the immediate; it seeks to find or to discover an authentication for all experience: past, present, and future.

Religious Experience

There are, of course, people who would deny that they have a need for religion. Often these are people who live for the moment, making the issues of meaning or purpose senseless. And there are those who deny that they have any natural drive toward the religious. These people are so absorbed in the successful business of everyday life that they have no time for ultimate questions. But the experience of the human race across time and culture, as well as the contemporary experience of many people, reveals a very different understanding. We humans, whether we want to admit it or not, are, in the final analysis, religious.

In the summer of 1978 a television documentary reported on a sampling of life as lived by some people in Marin County, California—a prosperous suburban community just across the Golden Gate Bridge from San Francisco. The report was principally an analysis of an unfeeling, self-centered group who pursued their own immediate pleasures with little concern for the future or for anyone else. It would not have been newsworthy if it has not been offensive to what most of us value: living for the future, living for others. Similarly, Colin M. Turnbull's analysis of a dislocated African tribe, the Ik, entitled *The Mountain People* (1972), was, as books on anthropology go, a best-seller. Why? Because Turnbull described the life-style of a people who, like those in the documentary about Marin County, abandoned their children, left the old to die uncomforted, and robbed the weak to satisfy their own momentary pleasure. We read the story of the Ik in fascinated horror, wondering how a people could move so far from those values we believe to be essential to life. Such values are ultimately religious.

Nevertheless, it is difficult to describe religious attitudes. In one sense religiousness is too personal and dynamic to be described analytically. But if we are to share and examine that which is deepest and most profound in our lives, it is essential to try.

One way that people have expressed their religiousness is by describing an experience of what can be best identified as the holy—that profound sense that there is infinitely more to experience than we can explain. The word "holy" points toward that which transcends or eludes comprehension, toward an awareness beyond our ordinary perceiving or conceiving. At best we can describe this awareness as mysterious, recalling that the word "mystery" expresses a sense of ignorance deeper than that which can be dispelled by information. Indeed, its proper referent is *radical* ignorance or that which we not only *do* not know, but *cannot* know through any usual means.

Human awareness of the religious stretches from records in painting and sculpture of the lives of early cave dwellers to the essays of contemporary theoretical scientists. Each describes in unique ways a dimension of life's experience that is best summarized in this way: If we look within ourselves we begin to see that our identity is dependent on something deeper than ourselves; it is like peeling away the layers of an onion—we eventually come to the inside; we find ourselves dependent upon that which is dependent upon nothing else; it is a feeling of absolute dependence in the presence of something which is of infinite worth or value.

It seems that the human mind is disposed not only to rationality, but also to spiritual awareness, an experience of both fascination and terror. When we acknowledge our ultimate finiteness and give over our lives to what is beyond our control, then we experience a sense of the sacred. To be con-

scious of ourselves as creatures before a creative force or
energy is to apprehend the religious dimension of life.

Another way people have described their religiousness is
by pointing to the basic assumptions upon which all human
life is lived. To be human is to assume that there is order in
the universe to be discovered, trusted, and accepted. When
the great nineteenth-century astronomer Joseph Leverrier
was confronted with what appeared to be meaningless irregularities in the orbit of the planet Uranus, his faith in the
basic order of the universe was so great that he asserted that
there had to be a reason for the irregularities. And so he went
looking for it, and discovered Pluto, a hitherto unknown
planet, which was causing the seemingly meaningless irregularities in the orbit of Uranus. The pursuit of life's order
is as natural as breathing. And despite life's seeming chaos
we discover with a resulting sense of awe and wonder that it
has order.

Some people have described their religiousness through a
discovery of the limits of language. We know that we are
only fully conscious of that which we can represent. Language is necessary to bring to full consciousness what we
experience. Yet as we try to express our experience of life's
meaning, we are aware that our consciousness points beyond the limits of our language—beyond what we can say or
imagine saying.

Over the last two hundred years Western civilization has
struggled to comprehend the human phenomenon. Through
the rise of the human sciences—psychology, sociology, eco-
nomics, political science, anthropology—we have attempted
to explain what being human is like. Our efforts have expanded our conscious knowledge greatly. But we still have
not really plumbed the depths of the unconscious. We do not
really understand what we were before we were born, and
death remains for humans the final unknown. We are like a
spot of brilliant light surrounded by the pitch black of our
ignorance. We cannot rest content with the light; we seek to
probe into the dark, to express what lies beyond our grasp.
The only language available to us is that of symbol or
metaphor (a figure of speech in which a word or phrase liter-

ally denoting one object or idea is used in place of another to suggest a likeness or analogy between them). To acknowledge the limits of our language makes us aware of our religiousness.

Our religiousness is that which is experienced in the midst of our humanness as the holy, that which is beyond expression except in the language of symbols, that which gives us a sense of order in the apparent chaos of life. Our religion provides us with a spiritual center of security and meaning; it provides roots of stability, coherence, and direction for our lives. Amid all our concerns, those concerns founded in religious faith demand a total surrender and, in return, promise to provide ultimate fulfillment. Destroy this center and most people are overcome by a radical anxiety. When a religious center is present, we possess hope and confidence—even in the most severe assault on life's meaning.

Two Types of Religion

This explanation of religion and the religious may seem somewhat confusing and even irrelevant to the vitality of the personal religious experience many people have and its resultant life-giving power. The purpose, however, in describing the human experience was to indicate the depth and breadth of religiousness as well as the necessity of vital religion in human culture. It is important to understand that living religiously is an attribute of personhood. However, what is perhaps more important is to acknowledge that this human longing for religious meaning can express itself in either negative or positive ways. Religion, while natural and necessary to human life, is not always in every expression to be valued or affirmed.

Religion has sometimes been attacked quite legitimately as supportive of what many people discern as the worst in human nature: intolerance, bigotry, sentimentality, self-righteousness, neurotic fantasy, rigidity, ignorance, and pride. At its worst religion, which should embody "perfect freedom," can become a form of slavery. Sociologists of religion have shown, for example, that unimaginative and restrictive "orthodoxy" (rigid adherence to the classical teachings of historic Christianity) can be linked to racism and a general insensitivity to human suffering. Suppression of the truth in the name of God has been all too common in human history. The question for some contemporary people is whether religion is a symptom of human sickness or necessary to our health.

It is important, therefore, to distinguish between two functional types of religion, one that is inclined to support health and one that is inclined to support sickness. Both make an appeal to ultimate goals. Both are beyond the limits of language and embodied in symbols. And both are perceived as holy. But they diverge quite radically and serve essentially conflicting functions in the lives of people and society. Ironically, both types of religion can be present in a single individual or in a single community. The first type of religion might be called "the religion of involvement" and the second type "the religion of escape."

THE RELIGION OF INVOLVEMENT

Religion can be a healthy response to life. When religion serves our human strengths, it is best understood as engaging us in life's struggles, as being rational, and as being expressive of inner control or self-direction.

A religion of involvement is dedicated to the pursuit of meaning and value in human life. Aware that the world can not meet our deepest needs, religion becomes an instrument for our progressive strivings after a sense of transcendent purpose for life. Just as important, it becomes a catalyst directing our lives toward a vision of a better life. It looks to the future and uses the past as leverage to move toward that future. Tradition is alive and provides a guide toward working with God to make creation anew.

There is no discomfort in the idea that God is a surprise. A religion of escape is easy; its demands are superficial; it gives the believer the illusion of safety. A religion of involvement is difficult and risky; its demands are profound; it points the pilgrim to a dark and dangerous road. It offers not safety but an opportunity to find new and unexpected maturity. Its adherents do not use the church and its liturgy for escape and comfort, but for challenge and empowerment. Their concern is not to judge or convert people who believe differently, but to live faithfully with them. Acknowledging their own acceptance and adequacy, their concerns are the world and the struggle for justice.

This type of religion meets the challenge of the intellect head-on. While it does not assert that one can know God by the power of one's mind, it certainly accepts reason and its cultivation as a gift of God. Beliefs are accepted only after they appear reasonable. These believers do not assume that there is a conclusive proof for the existence of God. Nor do they seek for a rational explanation of their experience which "explains" it all. They are simply aware that the more they push back the horizons of their knowing, the more aware they are of the infinite *more* to be explored.

They, therefore, live with a childlike openness to the *more* that lies beyond our perception and reason. They strive to perceive the subject that lies beyond their experience. For these open-minded people, reason and emotion, intellect and intuition, are all aspects of human life and essential for religious discovery. Still they seek to study seriously religion and the religious. And they subject their religious convictions to a thorough intellectual analysis.

As might be expected, these people are self-directed. While they do not know all the answers and do not have an authoritarian source for their beliefs, attitudes, and actions, they consciously strive to act morally. They have internalized norms for life consistent with their beliefs, and principles to be used as they rationally attempt to mediate between their norms and the moral situations in which they find themselves.

Someone who "has it all together," is one who we would say has a strong ego. Those with a "religion of involvement" have strong egos; they can face challenges, live in ambiguity and with change, and still maintain their equilibrium as they willingly move into the unknown as a necessary condition of growth. This does not mean that they are free from fear, but that they fear the numbing results of enslavement to the status quo more than they fear the change and uncertainty that go with personal and spiritual growth.

Such an understanding of religion is founded upon revelation rather than magic. Revelation is an openness to that which is hidden. It is the apprehension of experience as a whole, the affirmation of a fundamental power in society and nature for good, and the perception that life has an ultimate purpose. Religion as revelation is an invitation into fuller humanity, an attempt to bring human life into harmony with God's will rather than to manipulate the world for one's own benefit. It is the religion of a Dag Hammerskjold, a Martin Luther King, Jr., or a Dorothy Day.

The religion of involvement is an inclusive believing which takes the whole of human experience seriously. It draws and pushes us into the unknown that we may try to become that person who exists, truly, only in the mind of God. It provides the assurance which enables us to become vulnerable and to risk death. It fears no truth and is firmly convinced that truth is to be found in laboratories as well as churches, in the novels of atheists as well as in the lives of the saints. It despises nothing that God created and knows sin, not in terms of arbitrary labels, but in the uncertain light of what destroys our potential humanity. It insists that for religion there is no division of "sheep and goats" in terms of private and public, in-race and out-race, male or female, or rich and poor. It is a religion necessary for human health.

THE RELIGION OF ESCAPE

Some religion can serve human weakness. When it does, it is best understood as an escape from life, as an irrational emotional longing, and as an expression of an unconscious desire for parental authoritarianism.

For some people religion can be a support or protection from those dimensions of their lives in which they feel inadequate. Participation in the liturgy, while therapeutic, can be escapist, that is, it can make it possible to live with an unquestioned individual and social life. Membership in a prominent parish can give a person a sense of status and importance. To be offered multiple responsibilities in the church, regardless of their significance, is to acquire significance for oneself. If we are inclined to think of ourselves as inferior, a strict religious community with clear demands or beliefs that set us apart (no drinking, no dancing, and the like) can assure us that we are better than others if we are able to live up to those beliefs. At least we can be confident of a heavenly reward, which others, who may have "made it" in this life, cannot share.

These same people are typically unwilling to subject their religious convictions to intellectual analysis. Indeed, they often possess a strong anti-intellectual bias. They reject the question of whether or not their religious beliefs are reasonable. For them all that matters is a unique emotional experience. It is common for these people to hold the conviction that if people study religion seriously they will "lose their faith." A learned priest is someone to be avoided, as is serious adult education. These people typically protect themselves and their beliefs from attack and possible dissolution by resisting all logical scrutiny. Literalism, whether biblical, dogmatic, ethical, or liturgical, always seems to prevail among these close-minded adherents of fundamentalistic religion.

Further, those people with a "religion of escape" suffer from an unconscious wish for parental authoritarianism. They *know* the answers or have access to the answers because of an infallible authoritarian source which they project on God, the Bible, or the church. These people have often stopped growing at an emotional level in which they require an authoritarian parent to resolve the terror of life's uncertainty. God becomes a defense against the unknown, the conflicts and ambiguities of life. The very rigidity of such an authority is an assurance that they are safe.

Religion for these people is typically understood as magic or as the means by which they can achieve their desires by praying long and hard enough or by performing some other act of piety. It is a coercive, controlling, and manipulative vision of religion. Through the exercise of religion they seek to control life for their purposes. Through religious practices, they attempt to manipulate and control a parental authority through irrational means so they can cope with and control their essentially escapist world. It is in this sense that religion has sometimes been considered the "opiate of the people."

Clearly a religion of escape is defensive; it aims to protect one from alien forces. It is a safe harbor in a sea of storms. It comforts and provides peace of mind. Such a religion is functionally effective because it gives answers and leaves no questions. This also means that it is intolerant, moralistic, dogmatic, and rigid. Truth is known. One accepts it or rejects it; there is no continuing revelation. It is a religion of exclusion. It must by nature divide people into "we" and "they," at best considering the "they" as unenlightened and in error and at worst shunning and condemning them to hell. It supports bigotry, self-righteousness, repression, and even violence. Such a religion feeds on the need to be better than others and grows rapidly in times of uncertainty and cultural change. A religion of this sort can contribute to human (individual and corporate) sickness.

A Temptation and Challenge

Mature, healthy religion necessarily seeks a positive interaction between personal belief and the public world. It honors the hard work of critical examination, assuming that Christian believing is both plausible and reasonable. It desires to engage in intellectual analysis because it is convinced that this activity is necessary if the church is to be taken seriously and provide an effective moral witness to the world.

If we attempt to avoid the interaction between personal belief and the world, if we avoid engaging in conceptual thought aimed at enlightenment and action, then we are involved in an unjustifiable effort designed to mystify or bewilder. Healthy religion will always support and be expressive of mystery. But healthy religion will avoid that sense of false mystery, which sanctions our escape from the enigmas of life and from moral witness and which sick religion encourages.

Perhaps some illustrations of a false appeal to mystery will help. If we believe that God is all-powerful (can do anything), knows everything (even what will happen in 2000), and is everywhere, what do we make of such a tragic event as this? A couple has a daughter who is about to graduate from college with a 4.0 average. She is beautiful, active in the church, and has the promise of a very good job. A week before commencement she is killed in an automobile accident—hit by a drunk. The couple asks their priest, "How can an all-powerful, all-knowing, all-present God let this happen?" Well aware that to say, "It is God's will," is to make God out to be at best a kind of despot and, at worst, and more likely, a deranged monster, the priest replies, "The ways of God are a mystery." Such an answer refuses to deal with the doctrine of providence in today's world. Instead of examining, in the light of our contemporary understandings of appropriate moral behavior, the notion of free will, that of the girl who was killed, the drunken driver, and even that of the inventor of the internal combustion engine, the priest is *escaping* into a pseudo-mystery and is asking us to do the same.

For another example we can imagine a workshop on "experiental theology." In this workshop the leader, by means of music, meditative techniques, color slides, and body movement seeks to create a setting where we may come to a profound sense of God's presence in our lives. At the end of the exercise he says, "No one should talk to anyone else about what may have happened to him. Let us just 'live' this journey together into the symbolic world. The presence of God is always a mystery; to talk about it destroys the sense of this presence." Does it sound farfetched? Some have said that Christians should only dance their belief and avoid theological reflection. To put religious ideas in the form of theology, some believe, is to make belief meaningless and uninteresting. We would reply that in such a workshop setting a person may only have had, at best, an aesthetic experience. The only way such an experience can be distinguished from religious experience is by critical analysis.

A false appeal to mystery is always a temptation. For example: A priest might explain the heart of his or her parish ministry in this way. "We are an altar-centered parish. We come from all walks of life and every human condition. Every Sunday we gather about the Lord's table and eat the bread and drink the wine of the Lord. We look across at one another, and we find oneness. I do not ask what this means, because that will only divide us into theological camps. I just know that we have experienced the mystery that is God." There is something very appealing about this on one level: but what difference does it make on Monday morning? We need poetry in our religious lives, but we must also have prose. A false sense of mystery, while it may avoid arguments, also prevents us from dealing with the day-to-day implications of our belief.

In the first example, by ordinary standards an event is either purposeful, caused by the direct action of an agent, or else it is mere chance and illustrative of the absurdity of life. It means nothing to say it is a mystery. Theology has to face the darkness of death, not illuminate it artificially with platitudes that lie to our experience.

The leader of the workshop in the second illustration is suggesting that the meaning of religious experience wilts under the light of critical analysis. He, like the priest who wants to say it is just a mystery, believes that theology is alien to religious experience.

In the third illustration, the priest intentionally refuses to allow his ministry to go beyond the symbols and the story. In all of these illustrations, we see the tendency of false mystery to divide reality into the ordinary and the extraordinary, natural and supernatural, profane and sacred. This tendency leads ultimately to the division of private faith and public life. This division is contrary to the church's experience of Jesus.

Mystery is not to be removed from religion, only *false* mystery. Of course, the very nature of theology could be called a reduction into mystery. The believer who is thinking about God and humanity in a disciplined way—a good definition of theology—knows that the truth of anything said about God is conditioned upon our willingness to let that statement extend beyond our comprehension into the silent mystery of God. The silence, however, is not the answer, but the problem. We continue to probe that silence even though we understand that it is not possible for the finite to fully comprehend the infinite. Religion's positive interaction with the public world demands that we engage in a penetrating critical analysis of all our attempts to express in words and ideas our religious experience and faith.

· 2 ·

The Bible for Today's Church

- Do you read the Bible? How often and on what occasions?
- Have there been specific times in your life when a Bible passage has been especially helpful to you?
- We know that the Episcopal Church is not known as a "Bible church"—that is, it is not a church in which Bible preaching and a literal, ongoing interpretation of the Bible play the central role in worship. And yet the Bible plays a large role in the liturgical life of the Episcopal Church. What is one way of telling if a section of liturgy in the Book of Common Prayer has come from the Bible?

The Bible for Today's Church will help you answer these and many more questions about the Bible and the role it can or does play in your life. The volume attempts to set in perspective the Bible as a book and the Bible as the word of God. It also attempts to explain the different ways the Bible has been interpreted and understood at various points in its history. And, perhaps most important, it attempts to explain to contemporary Christians the living force the Bible *can* be in their lives.

Because Episcopalians have always had a special position in the mosaic of mainline Christianity, they have sometimes been a little confused about the role the Bible plays in their lives and worship. The churches of the Anglican Communion, the Episcopal Church among them, have elements of both the ancient Catholic tradition of the universal church and the newer Protestant tradition. The Catholic tradition places emphasis on the accumulated liturgical tradition of worship; the Protestant tradition places stronger emphasis on the authority of the Bible and Gospel preaching as the focal point of worship. The Episcopal Church sits between the two traditions. However, *The Bible for Today's Church* spells out the degree to which the Anglican liturgical tradition, as well as its tradition of literate Biblical preaching, are based solidly in Scripture.

The readings from this volume come from the beginning and end of the discussion. The first selection, "Why Read the Bible?" spells out exactly what meaning and practical purpose the Bible has for contemporary Christians. It also deals frankly with the difficulties and complexities of some Biblical interpretations and the ways they can and should be overcome.

The readings from the concluding section of the volume are very personal: they touch on the meditative and contemplative use of Scripture we all can make if we wish to do so. Three portions of a "Personal Study of the Bible" are included: "Acquiring the Tools" (what Bibles and other resource books you need for personal study); "Conversations with the Bible" (the valuable suggestions about how to set up an interior dialogue between yourself and the Bible you are reading); and "The Use of the Bible in Private Devotion" (outlining clearly the distinction between *Bible study* and the *devotional* use of the Bible). Each of these discussions concludes with a useful list of Further Reading. The authors, in these three discussions, have not spelled out a devotional program of Biblical centered spiritual exercises, because they believe such programs evolve from the needs of specific individuals. However, they have given some good guidelines for the journey.

Why Read the Bible?

Why read the Bible? At one level the answer is obvious. We have abundant statements on the subject, statements that vary from the private testimonials of satisfied users to the most authoritative of official pronouncements to the infinitely careful efforts of theologians to get the matter exactly right. All join in a mighty chorus to extol the values of reading the Bible.

A sample of these could begin with the Catechism in the Prayer Book:

> Q. Why do we call the Holy Scriptures the Word of God?
> A. We call them the Word of God because God inspired their human authors and because God still speaks to us through the Bible.

We could also look at an official statement that goes back to the time of the English Reformation. It comes from the Thirty-nine Articles of Religion that were framed to express, as tactfully as possible, our differences from the Calvinists on the one hand and the Roman Catholics on the other. In the sixth of these articles we read:

> Holy Scripture containeth all things necessary to salvation: so that whatsoever is not read therein, nor may be proved thereby, is not to be required of any man, that it should be believed as an article of Faith, or be thought requisite or necessary to salvation.

Next we could examine the rites by which bishops, priests, and deacons are ordained and see that everyone who is ordained signs a statement that attests:

> I solemnly declare that I do believe the Holy Scriptures of the Old and New Testaments to be the Word of God, and to contain all things necessary to salvation.

Indeed, we could look throughout the new Prayer Book and see that whenever the Bible is read the reader may conclude the lesson by saying, "The Word of the Lord," to which the response is, "Thanks be to God."

Such exalted claims about the Bible are not limited to official statements. Church history furnishes us with an abundance of individual Christians—great saints and ordinary churchmen, high officials in the church and laypeople, brilliant theologians and uneducated believers—who have combined in making superlative assertions about the value of Bible reading and study for their lives. Saint Augustine, for instance, referred to the Scriptures as "letters from home." And, something which gets closer to our own day, most of us have known some fellow Christians who have told us and others about how much time they spend with the Bible and of the guidance it gives to their lives and the joy it brings to their souls.

Why do we read the Bible? There is obviously no end of testimonials to the value of doing so, but these testimonials may be like letters of reference we have read about certain people: the extravagant words of praise are not consistent with our experience. Certainly they are not consistent with the experience of the majority of contemporary Christians. There is what has aptly been described as a "strange silence" of the Bible in the church. We continue to hear it read at most of our services, but we usually do not listen carefully and expectantly to what is being read. As for reading it ourselves on a regular basis for our own spiritual nourishment, either that is an idea that has never occurred to us, or we have tried it and, far from finding it helpful for understanding other things, we have not been able to make heads or tails of it. Or, if we did understand it, it seemed to tell us of a God who may have been all right in the bow-and-arrow league, but who sounded merely quaint in the role of creator and controller of a universe in which we can land a space ship on Mars and send television pictures back to earth from there.

A case in point for all of these difficulties may be found in the passage from Galatians 4:21–31 that was appointed to be read as the epistle for the Fourth Sunday in Lent in the 1928 Book of Common Prayer:

> Tell me, ye that desire to be under the law, do ye not hear the law? For it is written, that Abraham had two sons, the one by a bondmaid, the other by a freewoman. But he who was of the bondwoman was born after the flesh; but he of the freewoman was by promise. Which things are an allegory: for these are the two covenants; the one from the mount Sinai, which gendereth to bondage, which is Agar. For this Agar is mount Sinai in Arabia, and answereth to Jerusalem which now is, and is in bondage with her children. But Jerusalem which is above is free, which is the mother of us all. For it is written, Rejoice, thou barren that bearest not: break forth and cry, thou that travailest not: for the desolate hath many more children than she which hath an husband. Now we, brethren, as Isaac was, are the children of promise. But as then he that was born after the flesh persecuted him that was born after the Spirit, even so it is now. Nevertheless, what saith the scripture? Cast out the bondwoman and her son: for the son of the bondwoman shall not be heir with the son of the freewoman. So then, brethren, we are not children of the bondwoman, but of the free.

It is unlikely in the extreme that anyone who has ever heard that passage read in church has understood it without a great deal of study, much less felt that it immediately cleared up all of the unsolved mysteries of life. Merely to understand this passage from Galatians requires a good bit of background information. You have to know that it alludes to a story in Genesis 16 and 21 about Abraham, the ancestor of the people of Israel.

God had promised that he would be the ancestor of a great nation, but when Sarah his wife was well past her menopause and the possibility of any children at all began to look very remote, they decided to help God keep his promise. Sarah had a slave by the name of Hagar (the *h* was dropped off when the name was translated into the Greek of the New Testament). Sarah suggested that Abraham have his son by Hagar, a suggestion that was in accord with the customs of the time. After Hagar gave birth to a son named Ishmael, Sarah herself had a son who was called Isaac. Sarah then became very jealous for her son's inheritance and forced Abraham to drive Hagar and Ishmael out into the wilderness so that Hagar's son would not share Sarah's son's inheritance.

With that background information you can go on to see that in the passage from Galatians Paul sets up a series of equivalencies.

$$\frac{\text{Hagar}}{\text{Sarah}} = \frac{\text{mother after the flesh}}{\text{mother by promise}} = \frac{\text{old covenant}}{\text{new covenant}} = \frac{\text{earthly Jerusalem}}{\text{heavenly Jerusalem}}$$

The point of these equivalencies is to suggest that Christians are related to Jews as Isaac is related to Ishmael. This is to say that the church rather than Judaism is the true people of God and thus the church is the legitimate heir to all of God's promises to Israel.

It has taken this much effort merely to discover what point Paul was making. That says nothing about (a) whether the point is valid, and (b) what difference it makes to us. To establish its validity we would have to show that the true meaning of the story in Genesis did not have so much to do with Isaac and Ishmael as it did with Christians and Jews. We would have to go even further than that: the quotation that Paul makes toward the end of his argument, which begins, "Rejoice thou barren," is from Isaiah 54:1. A full validation would have to show that Isaiah also was talking about Christians and Jews in addition to Isaac and Ishmael.

Even assuming the soundness of Paul's argument, though, we are still left with the question of what difference it makes to us. It had never occurred to most of us to worry about whether Christians are the true people of God or not, so Paul's elaborate proof that we are answers a question that we did not ask.

Which brings us back to our original question: Why read the Bible? This whole book was written to answer that question and a closely related one: How do you read the Bible? While it takes the entire book to state that answer in full, a brief summary of it can be stated here.

Most of the Bible is narrative. Even the parts that are not, such as the writings of the prophets or the letters of St. Paul, are addressed to particular historical situations and have the function of dialogue in that history. Both individual Christians and the church as a body have discovered over the past 2,000 years what the people of Israel had discovered before them: when the people of God read these stories and try to discover the meaning of their own lives in the light of them, understanding comes. Through these stories they have felt that they heard God talking to them and telling them his will for them. Out of this experience they have come to regard the Bible as "the Word of God" and have been able to say, in the words of the Catechism, that "God still speaks to us through the Bible." Part of the purpose of this book is to see how this can be.

Obviously, not all Christians have had this experience of using the Bible to see their lives through God's eyes. That is why part of this book is on learning how to read the Bible; learning that can help remove impediments to the experience of hearing God speak through the Scriptures.

The section of the book that deals with how God can speak to us through the stories of the Bible is the second division of Chapter 4. Chapter 2 will be devoted to removing some impediments to reading the Bible by going over the process by which, from a human point of view, the Bible came into existence. The writing of the individual books, their recognition as Scripture, and their translation and transmission to us will be described as a way of discovering what kind of books they are.

Other impediments will be removed by a discussion of how the Bible has been interpreted in the past and how it is interpreted by scholars today. It will be seen that the purpose of most modern study techniques is to eliminate the sort of misunderstanding that arises from the differences between the historical and cultural circumstances of the world of the biblical stories and those of our own world.

Since it can no longer be expected that biblical stories will be familiar to Christian people, Chapters 5–7 will give a brief summary of them, together with a sketch of a modern understanding of the historical framework into which these stories are to be set. The beliefs about God and his people that are set forth in these stories will occupy Chapters 8–10. Finally, Chapter 11 will be devoted to situations in the church and home today in which the Bible is read and studied, and will make suggestions about how that can be done more effectively.

To summarize, then, the purpose of this book is not just to convey information about the Bible. Rather, it is written to help Christian people to read the Bible so that they can hear God speaking to them through its stories. We should admit in advance, however, that his voice is more easily discernible in some parts than in others. As it turns out, the passage we quoted from Galatians, in which Paul explains the relation of Christianity to Judaism in terms of the relation of Isaac to Ishmael, is not one of the stories that has the worst acoustics for hearing the Word of God. In fact, we will return to it again and again throughout the book to illustrate the principles that are being discussed. When you have gone through the whole book, it is our hope that you can hear God speaking to you through the Bible.

Acquiring Tools for Personal Bible Study

There are many reasons why a Christian might want to study the Bible: one could study in order to teach others, or the study might be a personal discipline undertaken for a particular season in the church year such as Advent or Lent, or it could be an ongoing effort to make oneself better informed as a Christian, or any of a number of other excellent reasons. The aim of Bible study is to hear more clearly what God revealed to the sacred writers and what he reveals through their words to us. To understand what the biblical authors wanted their original audiences to hear we focus on the biblical word within its historical and cultural context. Personal study strives to elucidate the historical or literal meaning of the words, passages, and stories of the Bible.

Only after we have learned what the words meant within their original context can we begin to examine what they might mean to us here and now.

Three major tools are necessary for success in this task: (a) the Bible itself, in at least two or three translations; (b) supporting secondary literature such as Bible dictionaries, commentaries, and other books on historical background and theological interpretation; and (c) one's own native intelligence and unaffected common sense which will put the right questions to the biblical text and trust the answers received to be the plain meaning of the text.

Selection between the many translations available today may be facilitated by reference to the discussion of them in chapter 1. Especially helpful are those editions that have explanatory articles and footnotes, such as the Oxford Annotated Bible (RSV), the Jerusalem Bible, the Annotated New English Bible, and the New American Bible. These different translations are needed by anyone not familiar with the Bible's original languages because no one translation can ever capture all of the nuances of the original. Having the same sentence phrased several different ways insures that we get the real point rather than something suggested by an accident of English phrasing.

The secondary literature is just that: secondary to the primary text which is the Bible itself. A good dictionary of the Bible is invaluable for identifying persons, places, objects, and concepts. Two publishers have issued good one-volume dictionaries, calling them, logically enough, *Harper's Bible Dictionary* and the *Westminster Dictionary of the Bible*. A singular accomplishment for one man is the *Dictionary of the Bible* written exclusively by John L. McKenzie. The standard multi-volume dictionary is *The Interpreter's Dictionary of the Bible* which began as four volumes and now has a supplementary volume to bring it up to date.

Commentaries give verse-by-verse interpretations of biblical books. There are two excellent single-volume commentaries on the entire Bible, *The Interpreter's One-Volume Commentary on the Bible* and *The Jerome Biblical Commentary*. In addition to the verse-by-verse analysis, both of these have valuable introductory essays on each biblical book as well as articles on biblical archaeology, geography, history, law, and so forth. The introductory essay should be read before one ever begins to study a biblical book in order to acquire an outline and overview of the book, as well as to learn its historical and theological background. The commentaries also include bibliographies that guide the reader to further and more detailed reading on the topics under consideration.

The most important tool after the text of Scripture itself is our own intelligence and common sense. That means that we approach the text with an open—but not an empty—mind. We let the plain meaning of the text come forth instead of imposing on the text what we think it ought to mean. This is to say that we must put aside our preconceptions in order to hear what the biblical writer is trying to say. This does not mean that we should approach the Bible without faith, but it does mean that we should approach it with a mind that is open to what is actually being said instead of with an expectation that it will confirm our opinions.

CONVERSATIONS WITH THE BIBLE

The best way of studying the Bible is to do so as though you are carrying on a dialogue with it. Better still, you should imagine youself as conducting an interview. You are holding a conversation with the text, putting questions to it and listening to its answers. The mystery of Bible study is that when we engage in it we enter into a dialogue not only with the words of the text but also with the divine-human encounter to which the words bear witness. Although we begin as the questioner, we soon find that we ourselves are called into question. Often our presuppositions are challenged. Rather than being frightened by this, we should accept it as a sign that we have begun to touch and to be touched by the divine Word.

Interviewing reporters proverbially ask five questions: who, what, when, where, and why. The Bible student must also ask five basic questions. The first is: What are the actual words of the passage? This is to ask whether we have the original text, what the author actually wrote. Finding this out is a highly technical process known as textual criticism (see above pp. 62–65). The amateur student of the Bible can make some decisions by seeing what variant readings are mentioned in the footnotes of the various translations and in the commentaries.

The second question to be put to the text is: What are the literary boundaries that make this passage a distinct unit, or *pericope*, to use the technical term? In other words, how does this passage fit into the outline of the book? Just as a bone can only be understood as part of a skeleton, so a passage must be seen as part of the argument of the whole book. To outline the book we note the chief characters and the progress of the action. Then we see where our bit fits in. If the passage is not narrative but, for instance, a collection of laws or proverbs, we ask what they have in common with one another, what holds them together as a unit.

Our third question concerns the identity of the speaker and the audience. Who is speaking here, to whom does he speak and for what purpose? It is important to find out not only the author's name, but where he comes from and what tradition or point of view he represents. Priests, prophets, kings, sages, and poets all speak different languages and use the literary devices that are common to their "trade." Their audience can also differ. The way a priest addresses the worshipers in the Temple is not the way a prophet speaks to a crowd, a king addresses his subjects, or a teacher talks to pupils. The help this identification of the speaker gives in understanding the passage is like the help we get from knowing whether a scene we see on television is from a newscast, a situation comedy, a dramatic story, or a commercial. The sense we make of it will depend on the purpose for which we think it is being used.

The fourth question is: What did the words of the text mean in their original historical and cultural context? Here the questioner is asking what the words or unit meant in the plain language of the time. The focus is on the literal meaning of the words, phrases, and concepts of the passage at the time it was written.

Finally, our dialogue with the text asks the last question: How was the original plain meaning of the text used later on within the Bible itself and within the Judeo-Christian tradition in the years since? In this way we can come to ask what the text means today. The Bible, as God's living word, means more than its original, historical meaning. This is shown by the retelling of patriarchal stories, the reuse prophets made of older prophecies, and the New Testament recycling of the Hebrew Bible. Each generation hears God's word anew for its own time and circumstances. For contemporary Christians who are products of the historical consciousness of today, the more-than-literal meaning of the Bible can only be sought after one is thoroughly familiar with the plain historical meaning. We cannot step out of our time and place and resort to a timeless sphere where truths are eternal and unconditioned by historical concreteness.

The personal study of the Bible through this question and answer exercise seeks to open our hearts to the inner power and dynamic of the written Word of God. These steps take us from the original meaning to the present meaning of the text. Because God continually reveals his will to his people, we cannot be satisfied with what we assume the Bible is saying to us today. We must seek to test and enrich the word today with what it meant when it was first uttered and when used through the generations.

FOR FURTHER READING:

Aldrich, Ella V., and Camp, Thomas E. *Using Theological Books and Libraries.* Englewood Cliffs, N.J.: Prentice-Hall, Inc., 1963. A valuable guide on how to use a theological library, with comment on the different types and particular titles of books related to Bible study.

Brown, Robert McAfee. *The Bible Speaks to You.* Philadelphia: Westminster Press, 1955. An excellent effort to draw on historical criticism as a way of showing how the theological and moral themes of the Bible speak to young people—and adults—today.

Brueggemann, W. *The Bible Makes Sense.* Atlanta: John Knox Press, 1977. A particularly useful way of getting into the theological thought world of the Bible. It is a "how to" book dealing with the major biblical themes.

Griffin, William Augustus. *Who Do Men Say That I Am?*, Atlanta: Episcopal Radio-TV Foundation, 1972. Two cassettes with a study guide on understanding Jesus in the light of the Old Testament.

Interpretation (A Journal of Bible and Theology), vol. 32 no. 2 (April, 1978). Richmond: Union Theological Seminary in Virginia. This issue of *Interpretation* has several helpful articles on recent Bible translations, useful in comparing the different translations one might use in studying the Bible.

Kaiser, Otto and Kümmel, Werner. *Exegetical Method: A Student's Handbook.* New York: Seabury Press, 1963. A quite practical guide to the method and resources used in studying the Bible. It presupposes that one intends to be a "serious" student of the Bible.

Richardson, Alan, ed. *A Theological Word Book of the Bible.* New York: Macmillan Co., 1950. A useful dictionary-like guide to the theological meaning of terms and concepts.

Verna Dozier is also involved in publishing a cassette presentation on group Bible study for the Episcopal Radio-TV Foundation. It will include a concise summary of the story of the Bible.

The entire King James translation of the Bible has been recorded by Alexander Scourby in sixty-four cassettes for the Episcopal Radio-TV Foundation. The cassettes may be ordered individually, in volumes, or by the entire set.

The Use of the Bible in Private Devotion

The Bible has been at the heart of personal spirituality for many centuries. A number of the psalms, for instance, were written to express the joy of meditating on the Torah day and night. The beginnings of the Christian monastic movement in the Egyptian desert centered around hermits who memorized all of the psalms and filled their days by reciting them. Translations of the Bible into the languages of the people at the time of the Reformation began a strong tradition of lay spirituality that focused on daily Bible reading.

At the same time it must be said that many Christians who have wanted to grow closer to God have set out earnestly on an effort to read the Bible only to become bogged down and discouraged, feeling that they were somehow left outside of an experience that must be reserved for the privileged few.

Sometimes they began with an intention of reading the Bible straight through, "from cover to cover," as the expression goes. This effort may not have lasted past the fifth chapter of Genesis, which is filled with sentences like: "And Mahalaleel lived sixty and five years and begat Jared: and Mahalaleel lived after he begat Jared eight hundred and thirty years, and begat sons and daughters: and all of the days of Mahalaleel were eight hundred ninety and five years: and he died" (Gen. 5:15–17). Whether this or something else happened, they decided that the Bible would have to remain a closed book to them.

Most people would be well advised to get into devotional reading of the Bible on a more modest scale at the beginning than setting out to read all of it straight through. The use of a daily devotional guide that has a Scripture reading of a few verses for each day is a good way to get one's feet wet. *Forward Day by Day*, which is available on the tract racks of most parish churches, is a very good example of this sort of thing. One of its strongest advocates was Duke Ellington:

> Ever since I saw the first copy, this little book has been my daily reading. It is clear, easy to understand, written in the language of the ordinary man, and always says things I want to know. (*Music Is My Mistress*, p. 282)

The British-based Bible Reading Fellowship, with American headquarters at Post Office Box M, Winter Park, Florida 32789, publishes daily Bible study guides (Series A Notes) and a daily inspirational booklet called *Salt*. At the time of this writing, both of these plus three books of Christian interest and a newsletter can be ordered from the address above for six dollars per year. This combination is referred to as the "Compass" program.

When one feels ready to try reading the Bible book by book, there are better sequences in which to read than straight through from beginning to end. Since Christians understand the Old Testament through the New, the best place to begin is with the life of Jesus in the Gospel according to Mark. After that it is good to look at the history of the early church in Acts. A few letters of St. Paul may be read after that. One may then turn to Exodus in the Old Testament, Joshua, Judges, 1 and 2 Samuel, and 1 and 2 Kings. After that possibly Amos, Hosea, and Isaiah or Jeremiah. One's own interest will· probably be a safe guide after that.

The distinction between Bible study and devotional reading must be remembered. The intention is not so much historical understanding as it is to apply the Bible to one's own life, to engage one's feelings in response to God's Word and his mighty acts. A suggestion that was made by Bishop John Coburn in relation to the prayers of the Bible can be transferred to all devotional reading of the Scriptures: make the readings your own by reading them slowly as if they were addressed to you. This can be done in the Psalms, for instance, by emphasizing all of the pronouns in the first person, as in Psalm 23 in the new Prayer Book:

The Lord is *my* shepherd;
   I shall not be in want.
He makes *me* lie down in green pastures
   and leads *me* beside still waters.
He revives *my* soul
   and guides *me* along right pathways for his Name's sake.

The letters of Paul can be read as though you were a member of the congregation to whom they were written. Sometimes scholars use two Latin terms to refer to two senses of Scripture. They speak of the meaning *extra nos*, "outside of us," which is the objective and historical meaning. They also speak of the meaning *pro nobis*, "for us," which is the subjective and devotional meaning. The two do not always have to be closely related. One does not really have to be convinced that Jesus calmed a storm at sea in order to believe that he can bring peace to our tempestuous lives.

From this effort to make the readings our own to what is technically described as meditation is but a short step. Meditation is an exercise of spiritual response to a passage from the Bible, especially a story from the life of Jesus. The exercise has three steps which have been variously designated by different writers. Bishop Coburn lists the steps this way:

1. To *picture* a Biblical scene,
2. To *ponder* its meaning,
3. To *promise* God something as a result.

The Presiding Bishop, on the other hand, has spoken of these three steps as God in my head, God in my heart, and God in my hands. The first step is to recreate the scene imaginatively. One technique is to imagine that you were one of the characters in the story and think how you would tell what happened to someone else. The next step is to ask what the story means, what God was trying to do, what he is saying to you through the story. Finally, you commit yourself to a concrete action, no matter how small, to implement what you have gained from the meditation.

Sometimes meditation can be done in a group. One particular method has been recommended by Walter Wink. He suggests that members of the group do homework on the historical criticism of the passage and begin their session by discussing the passage exegetically. After that the members of the group try to picture the scene. The next step, which is very effective, draws on a technique used by psychoanalysts trained in the methods of Carl Jung. In the Jungian treatment of dreams the dreamer is not identified exclusively with the self in the dream; each character of the dream is thought to represent one dynamic of the subject's personality. Transferred to group meditation on the Bible, the technique enables members of a group reflecting, for example, on the parable of the Healing of the Paralytic to see that parts of themselves have been healed by Christ as the paralytic was, while other parts of themselves are more like the scribe who objects that the healing was performed on the Sabbath.

In devotional use of the Bible Christians can hear God speaking to them through his Word more directly than almost any other way.

FOR FURTHER READING:

Coburn, John B. *Prayer and Personal Religion.* Layman's Theological Library. Philadelphia: The Westminster Press, 1957. A good simple introduction to the various forms of prayer.

de Dietrich, Suzanne. *Discovering the Bible*. Nashville: Source Publishers, 1953. Both a theoretical and a practical guide for meditation upon Scripture.

————. *God's Unfolding Purpose: A Guide to the Study of the Bible*. Philadelphia: The Westminster Press, 1960. Provides an overall sweep of the biblical drama together with a section-by-section guide to the study of and meditation upon the Bible.

Robertson, E. H. *"Take and Read": A Guide to Group Bible Study*. London: SCM Press, 1961. Examines different types of group Bible study and suggests which are most appropriate for particular kinds of groups. Included is a chapter on how to choose a biblical book for study.

Wink, Walter. *The Bible in Human Transformation: Toward a New Paradigm for Biblical Study*. Philadelphia: Fortress Press, 1973. This book not only sets forth the method of group meditation described above but also gives a trenchant analysis of how biblical study has been subverted from a means of religious growth into an academic discipline with no personal implications.

· 3 ·

The Church in History

- What role has the history of your own family played in your life? How are you different from your grandparents? Your own parents? How are you the same?
- What historic moments in the unfolding of the Christian story have you witnessed?
- Who are the persons who have had the greatest impact on your life to date? Have they only had impact on your life or have they played a part in other people's lives as well?
- What historical figure has had the greatest impact on your life? Really *think* about this one—we meet many people through our learning and reading.

The Church in History has a very simple and strong message about the importance of studying the history of the Christian church. In fact, the author believes that the most basic and important reason for studying any history is to learn the lessons the past has to teach us and to locate ourselves in the great web of human history and in the history of the relationship of God to the human race. The volume traces the evolution of the Christian church from its earliest days to very recent times. The author's unique and dramatic approach is to tie the events of certain crucial periods in the history of the Christian church to the lives of believers. The stories are both intimate and upsetting at times, but they ring with the truth of the idea that history is us.

35

The first two selections—"Why Study History?" and "Why Study Church History"—are from the first section of the book and are the basic equipment we need to begin our renewed awareness of the past and its messages for us. The third selection is upsetting because it hits so close to our own lifetime and the events of the world around us. It is the moving story of the martyrdom in 1977 of Janani Luwum, the Anglican Archbishop of Uganda, in Africa, at the hands of the secular government of his country. The chapter is entitled "Four Themes and One Person: Janani Luwum." It tells in the most dramatic and heartbreaking—yet triumphant—way that Christianity is still happening, that the martyrs of the Christian faith were not "used up" by the gladiatorial contests of ancient Rome and the religious wars of Europe's past. It lifts off the image of church history as something contained in a dusty and boring book found on the most obscure shelf in the library, and beneath that image we find the daily newspaper and a weekly news magazine.

Having read all of the sections provided here, you might consider the story of your own life once more. If your life were to be committed to paper right now, would you be pleased or upset by the story it told? In what ways could you change history—your own or the history of your immediate community—by your actions? It is unlikely that you will come away from the reading of this group of selections with quite the same view of history you had before you read them.

The Importance of Church History for Ourselves and for the Community

Why Study History?

We study history because we must if we are to be fully human.

How can such a sweeping claim be understood? We begin by confronting the fact that we are social beings. Aristotle, in the fourth century before Christ, wrote of the origins of the political community, the state. It all began with the necessary union of male and female for the perpetuation of humanity. There followed the association of people in families, in villages, in cities, and in nations. Thus the history of humanity began.

That which is true of our origins is emphatically true of our present condition. John Donne, writing in the seventeenth century as Dean of St. Paul's Cathedral, London, affirmed:

> No man is an island, entire of itself; every man is a piece of the continent, a part of the main. If a clod be washed away by the sea, Europe is the less, as well as if a promontory were, as well as if a man of thy friend's or of thine own were: any man's death diminishes me, because I am involved in mankind, and therefore do not send to me to know for whom the bell tolls; it tolls for thee.

This involvement in mankind is not limited to space. It embraces time as well. Thus if Donne were living now he might, possibly, write:

"No man is a moment or a lifetime, entire of itself; everyone is a part of the whole, of time past, time present, and time yet to come. What Galileo saw and understood as he looked through his telescope—Alaric the Goth's sack of Rome, Lee Harvey Oswald's assassination of a President—all impinge on my life: Anyone's death, now, in time past, in time to come, diminishes me, because I am involved in mankind, and therefore do not send to me to know for whom the bell tolls; it tolls for thee."

Galileo's discoveries concerning the nature of the universe involved the death of a world view which had dominated human perceptions for centuries. Because he seemed to be turning the truth upside down, his discoveries aroused the ire of the church hierarchy. Alaric's sack of Rome is a symbol of the end of the Roman peace and of Roman domination of the Mediterranean world. But the event is also symbolic of the release of new possibilities, prospects which led to the development of Western Europe with its achievements and failures. Lee Harvey Oswald's fatal shooting of President Kennedy involved the death of hope for many people and a reassessment of ourselves and our corporate life in the latter half of the twentieth century. Such events in time past impinge on us now. We are involved in mankind through the ages. If we are to know who we are we must self-consciously relate ourselves to the past.

We are here engaged in understanding time and our relationship to time. We are probing the mystery of time. In such probing we may expect to discover something about our human nature which we might otherwise ignore. Indeed, because consideration of things past involves work and pain as well as entertainment and fulfillment we are inclined to deny the significance of the past. That we must not, cannot do so was the conviction of Charles Henry Brent, modern missionary, bishop, and statesman of the Episcopal Church. He once referred to a Scottish philosopher, whom he did not name, who asserted that the chief characteristic of time was "its togetherness."[2] Past, present, and future are interrelated. It is true of the individual whose personal history is involved in what we will and do at present. It is also true of society whose corporate history through centuries of human experience is involved in our present social policies and in their application. Furthermore, if we ignore history we deteriorate, becoming less than fully human. If we refuse to study the past, we abdicate from the power and authority, which we rightly possess, over the historical forces that impinge upon us, and we are in grave danger of being led like dumb oxen into the future. There are strong tendencies within us, as individuals and as groups, to conform to the dominant intellectual, moral, and cultural trends of the present age, without thought, without criticism, and without control.

As humans we are gifted with that which Ortega y Gasset, the Spanish philosopher, has called the historical sense. This is the "sense" by which we perceive the past, and traveling away from ourselves into that past we gain necessary perspective on the present. If we exercise this sense we will gain the leverage needed to break away from the forces of this age which seek to control us, and we will regain our lost humanity. We will also be better prepared to move creatively into the future.

Some people might protest that the study of history often involves an irresponsible flight from present responsibilities. The study of history has also been used to buttress unwarranted, destructive authority in government, religion, art, and science. There is no denying the fact that historical studies can and will be used and abused in the service of base and dehumanizing motives. Historical study needs to be examined critically in order to discern the prejudices and presuppositions of its practitioners. When historical investigation is pursued with the utmost seriousness, the historical sense with which we are endowed works against all abuse and is a means by which we are protected against tyrannical power. Historical study as a rigorous, critical discipline exercised on behalf of humanity, its dignity and freedom, is essential to our well-being and indeed to our survival. This is a fact attested to by the psychiatrist who assists patients to recover their pasts in order that they may find themselves. It is a fact understood by the wise world leader who, for the sake of sanity and survival, will not let anyone forget the horrors of the Nazi death camps, the tragic nightmare of Hiroshima, and the napalm deaths in Vietnam.

Why Study Church History?

We study church history because we are human beings and possess an historical sense. We are involved in mankind. The church as a part of society shares history with those who stand apart from the church. But there is more to the answer than this.

Christianity by its very nature is concerned for history. Unlike others of the world religions, its roots are in historical events which are of the greatest significance. It is composed of the followers of Jesus Christ who we affirm was

> born of the Virgin Mary.
> He suffered under Pontius Pilate,
>   was crucified, died, and was buried.
> He descended to the dead.
> On the third day he rose again.

To be a Christian is to remember the historical Jesus and that which God did through him here on earth, among particular women and children and men. This remembering is not antiquarian in nature, nor is it meant to bolster present church authority. It is not static or passive. The remembering involves experiencing the presence of Christ *now* by the power of the Holy Spirit. As Scripture is read and the Word of God preached, as the Creed is said and the faithful join in Holy Communion, Christians participate in Christ. This is what is meant by the Eternal Present and it has roots in the Hebrew mode of remembering.

In the Book of Deuteronomy (26:5–8) a liturgy is given for the presentation of the firstfruits at the central sanctuary of Israel. Here God's mercies are recounted, and as they are, that which was past is present, the "he" becomes "us":

And you shall make response before the Lord your God, "A
wandering Aramean was my father; and he went down into
Egypt and sojourned there, few in number; and there he became a nation, great, mighty, and populous. And the Egyptians
treated us harshly, and afflicted us, and laid upon us hard bondage. Then we creid to the Lord the God of our fathers . . . and
the Lord brought us out of Egypt. . . .

In a similar manner, as Christians remembered their Lord
he was in the midst of them. The barrier of time was overcome in the act of thanksgiving which is remembering.

To be a Christian is to remember events on both sides of
the central events of God in Christ on earth. God worked
through his chosen people, Israel. God works through his
chosen people, the New Israel, the Christian community. We
remember thus because faith affirms that God the Creator has
been God the Redeemer of his marred and fallen creation
from the beginning of time. The temporal reality—under
Pontius Pilate—is Eternal Fact. Thus twentieth-century
Christians understand that they are involved in the Old Israel: it is their history. Anti-Semitism is rejected. Twentieth-
century Christians are also involved in the centuries of
triumph and tragedy of the church: it is their history. Remembering the course of events from the beginning until
now, with the center of history in the historic Jesus illuminating that which went before and that which followed after,
Christians derive wisdom and power and inspiration to carry
on. They are enabled to carry on that which makes effective
the mission of Christ and to break loose from the past as it
inhibits that mission of salvation for all peoples.

Remembering, in the dynamic manner which we have
been considering, constitutes the primary vocation of the
church. Remembering is the chief activity of Christians, for
remembering involves action guided and empowered by the
Holy Spirit. Remembering is a mode of worship which im-
pels the worshiper to represent Christ in the world as the
agent of justice and love.

Even this is not all that must be said. The study of church
history is important not only for the reasons given above, but
also because such study arouses a sense of the distance and
the difference between past and present. This understanding

of distance and difference has been of very great importance since, as some scholars believe, it was first introduced by humanists of the fourteenth and fifteenth centuries in Western Europe. It was among the roots of the Reformation of the sixteenth century. Martin Luther and others perceived how different the church they knew in the sixteenth century was from the church of the Apostles and their followers in the first and second centuries. Observing the difference, they sought to reform their decadent and corrupt church according to the example of the earliest church. This understanding of distance and difference can also be found at the roots of the nineteenth-century Anglo-Catholic objection to the Reformation. Hurrell Froude, the friend of John Henry Newman, was most vehement in his denunciation of the reformers, sensing the distance between them and the Middle Ages which he so much admired. A sense of distance and difference from the past, whether expressed through admiration or disgust, is vital for the most fruitful and honest study of history.

Some students of history resist awareness of distance and difference. They demand that everything be put in their own terms so that they may immediately understand and dominate the past. They prefer those who simply recite facts or those who fictionalize history, dressing it up with modern language and attitudes. The differences between past and present are glossed over or obliterated. Even those who understand the importance of remembering may be inclined to this error. To remember Jesus is not to make him one of us. A distance remains; there is a difference between him and us. Likewise, church history is not composed of an endless series of stories which can be used to embellish otherwise dull sermons, pointing out how Augustine or Calvin or Niebuhr thought as we do about this or that. A part of the community of saints, Augustine of Hippo remains a fifth-century bishop of a North African church. There is great distance and difference, in time, space, and basic attitudes, between Augustine and ourselves. To be a student of history in the best sense is to be conscious of historical distances and differences.

It is important, for instance, to realize that the way a person in ancient Rome perceived reality differs greatly from our own perceptions. We take for granted many things which would be incomprehensible to someone in the ancient world. Sigmund Freud's recovery of the unconscious, Charles Darwin's exposition of the evolution of species by means of natural selection, and the discovery of the place of planet earth not at the center of the universe but as a tiny speck rotating around a star which is one among countless numbers of stars—these commonplaces of the modern perception of reality were unknown in sixteenth-century England and in first-century Rome.

Consider for a moment the fact that early Christians viewed the world and humanity at the center of the universe surrounded by spheres at the outer limit of which there was located heaven, where God and the saints dwelt. This is not how we understand the universe, nor can it be, although we cannot say that the way we view it is final in the sense that it will never be modified. Nevertheless, we act on the basis of our understanding of earth as a planet of the sun, the sun as one among millions, the universe limitless.

This difference of perception has, as might be expected, ramifications. For one thing, under the old view God inhabited a place—up there! Now there are serious discussions concerning where God is, if he is anywhere. The modern understanding of God's location is inclined to be abstract and to seek for God, for instance, in the depth of being. Then, too, under the old view the way of salvation was likened to an ascent up a ladder. It has been pictured in terms of a ladder extending up from earth through the rotating spheres to God's heaven. Along the way evil spirits retard while angels assist the pilgrim up the ladder of perfection. The Christian life was thus a pilgrimage, involving the gradual perfection of the saints through prayers and good deeds. Our perception of reality influences our understanding of the Christian life. It is vitally important that we be aware of differing perceptions, realizing the distance which separates us from the past. Being thus sensitive to the differences we shall be better able to study, to criticize, to evaluate, and to learn. We shall also be better equipped to remember that which ought to be remembered and to forget that which ought to be forgotten.

For this reason—that the reader may have some sense of historical distance—there will be words and ideas in the following chapters which seem strange and are at first difficult to understand. You may ask why there are so many quotations, why some of them are so long, and why they aren't put into the author's words instead. The answer is that I want the reader to be constantly reminded of the distance and thus be enabled time and again to encounter the past, not as we would have it but as it was. You are asked, therefore, to *work* through this book, not skipping the quotations because they are difficult, letting them and the interpretations of them sink in until you feel the distance between then and now. Once the distance is sensed, the encounter with the past begins and you will find yourself passing beyond the differences to experience that lively remembering which enriches humanity and faith.

The effort required in reading church history brings rewards as dialogues occur between the reader and the past. Princess Elizabeth of Hungary, Saint Elizabeth, is remembered for the sacrificial care she provided for the sick in the thirteenth century. Thomas More, Lord Chancellor of England in the sixteenth century, has been immortalized as "the man for all seasons" and is remembered for his struggle to remain true to his conscience as his patriotism was being tested. Both saints were in the world and both possessed ample supplies of grace and good humor, Elizabeth entertaining her court, Thomas entertaining his friends in his lively household. Both wore hair shirts, shirts made of haircloth and worn by ascetics and penitents. The shirt worn next to the skin, irritated the flesh and was sometimes painful. Why did they wear such a thing? Were they masochists? Consider the fact seriously and you enter into another world, one far different from that which is familiar to most twentieth-century Americans. It is a world where the scourging of the body is not evidence of mental distress or illness but of health, sanity, and holiness. For unlike the majority of persons who worship before mirrors and live for the sake of the belly and of vanity, Elizabeth of Hungary and Thomas More sought to subdue the body that they might live for God and for those for whom the Lord Christ died on the cross. The hair shirt was an ally, beneficent and good. It did not put an end to their good humors. Instead, it supported them.

Here is something to consider, to wrestle with: persons become more real to us as we realize their otherness. Indeed we might find ourselves learning from them how to love, how to live in obedience to the Lord.

Note

1. John Donne, *Devotions upon Emergent Occasions* (Meditation 17) (Ann Arbor, Mich.: University of Michigan Press, 1959), pp. 108–9.

2. Charles Henry Brent, *The Commonwealth: Its Foundations and Pillars* (New York: Appleton, 1930), p. 22.

The Church in History: Concluding Reflections

Four Themes and One Person: Janani Luwum

The themes and issues come together forcefully in the martyrdom of Janani Luwum, Archbishop of Uganda, Rwanda, Burundi, and Boga-Zaire in East Africa. Archbishop Luwum was the spiritual leader of more than three million Christians in a population of about eleven million Ugandans. His church, with at least as many members as the Episcopal Church in the United States, if not more, has been steadily and dramatically growing while Anglican churches elsewhere have been shrinking. This is due in part to the strong tradition of evangelism in East Africa, but also in part to the inspired leadership which has led to the forming of a church in which the people with a great variety of gifts have been engaged in the vital functions of the Christian community. In the diocese of Kigezi, for instance, there are more than 700 congregations but only fifty salaried priests. Basic to the church's operation are the lay ministers, trained on the basis of their discerned, individual gifts to be teachers, pastors, evangelists, prophets, healers, and who would not wish to receive money for their ministries. The church in East Africa has been likened to that of the Book of Acts, so full of the Spirit and so vibrant its members. East African Christians help to account for the fact that the majority of Anglicans in the world today are nonwhites.

In part the spirit of the East African church is derived from and contributes to the heroic witness of its members throughout its history. The martyrdom of Bishop James Hannington and his companions at the hands of King Mwanga in 1885 is remembered. Further martyrdoms occurred, involving both Roman Catholics and Anglicans. But the church's mission did not end. Indeed, "the blood of the martyrs" was "the seed of the church." Now there is a new ruler in Uganda and there are new martyrs, one of them being Janani Luwum.

As is true of most martyrdoms, the archbishop's resembles the passion of the Lord. First of all, he was falsely accused of conspiring to overthrow the government. In Janani's own words, written just days before his death:

> At about 1:30 A.M. on Saturday morning [February 5, 1977] I heard the dog barking wildly and the fence being broken down, and I knew some people had come into the compound. I walked downstairs very quietly without switching any lights on and, as usual, I stopped at the door. I opened the curtain on the door on one side and I was able to observe one man standing straight in front of the door. He began calling "Archbishop, Archbishop, open! We have come!" This man was called Ben Ongom. Because he had some cuts on his face and I knew him in the past, I thought he was in some kind of danger needing help. So I opened the door and immediately three armed men who had been hiding sprang on me, cocking their rifles and shouting, "Archbishop, Archbishop, show us the arms!" I replied, "What arms?" They replied, "There are arms in this house." I said, "No." At this point their leader who was speaking in Arabic and wearing a red kaunda suit put his rifle in my stomach on the right hand side whilst another man searched me from head to foot. He pushed me with the rifle, shouting, "Walk! Run! Show us the arms! . . . ."[1]

Thus a night of terror began. No arms were found in the house or on the grounds. The archbishop had reason to believe that he was being associated with a political coup in which he was not involved and knew nothing about.

His Excellency Al-Hajji Field Marshall Dr. Idi Amin Dada,

life president of Uganda, with leaders from his own Kakwa tribe, had decided to eradicate his enemies in the Acholi and Langi tribes, both of which had ties with Amin's predecessor Milton Obote and with many of the country's intellectuals and clergy. Janani came from the Acholi tribe and was regarded as a possible if not actual enemy of the president. In addition, the archbishop and his bishops were neither radical revolutionaries nor passive followers of Amin. In their letter protesting the unlawful search of the archbishop's house, the bishops stated:

> Your excellency, our Church does not believe nor does it teach its members the use of destructive weapons. We believe in the Life-giving love of Christ, we proclaim that love to all without fear—as your Excellency knows. We speak publicly and in private against all evil, all corruption, all misuse of power, all maltreatment of human beings. We rejoice in the truth, because truth builds up a nation, but we are determined to refuse all falsehood, all false accusations which damage the lives of our people and spoil the image of our country.[2]

At the end of the letter, concerned for the tarnished image of their country brought on by recurrent bloodshed, they boldly said: "Our advice, Your Excellency, is that you put your Intelligence under strict laws in their work, restore authority to the Police, and let the law replace the gun—then the image will be restored."

At the next stage of the developing drama we find the archbishop on trial. For days the bishops sought for an audience with President Amin and for days were put off. Finally, on Tuesday, February 15, they were summoned with all religious leaders—including Roman Catholics and Muslims—to the Government Conference Center in Kampala. On the same day Radio Uganda reported that arms had been found near the archbishop's house. The next day, Wednesday, February 16, at 9:30 in the morning, the bishops arrived outside the Conference Center to find almost all of the Uganda army present—one source reports that there were 3,000 heavily armed troops there—with all government officials, excepting President Amin, and with all of those accused of conspiracy to overthrow the government.

Accusations were made again, arms were displayed, confessions were read out implicating the archbishop and two government officials in the supposed plot. As the archbishop's name was read he was seen to shake his head in disbelief and denial. The trial—for such it was—went on for hours, the crowd being harangued into a frenzy. Finally, the vice-president of Uganda, General Mustafa Adrisi, cried out, "What do you think? What should we do with these people?" The troops shouted, "Kill them! Kill them now!" A vote was taken and all the soldiers voted for death.

The bishops then entered the Conference Center expecting an audience with Amin, but all the religious leaders were dismissed, with the exception of the archbishop, who was detained. Other sources say that Janani was arrested by Muslim Military Police and driven off to the Nakasero lodge for his meeting with the president. This was the last that Festo Kivingere, bishop of Kigezi saw of Janani.[3]

The third act in the drama concerns Archbishop Luwum's death by execution. We cannot be absolutely certain concerning the specific details of his death, except to say that the government's story was a lie. He and the two government officials accused with him were reported to have been killed in a car accident as they attempted to overpower the driver. But the car pictured by the Ugandan press was recognized as one involved in an accident two weeks earlier. Furthermore, witnesses came forward to testify to seeing the archbishop's body riddled with bullet holes. One eyewitness account has been given by Janani's driver, who managed to escape across the border into Tanzania.[4] The archbishop, we are informed, was brought handcuffed before President Amin at the Nakasero lodge. Janani was asked to sign a document confessing his part in the conspiracy. He refused. He was ordered to kneel before the president and beg forgiveness. Again he refused. Amin then sent for troops who pinned the archbishop to the floor, stripped him of his cassock and gold cross and then of all his clothes and whipped him. While he was being thus scourged Janani prayed. His prayers aroused the president who shouted obscenities at him and struck him. Once more he was ordered to sign the document and beg for forgiveness, but Janani refused, now calm and stead-fast. Amin then began to speak of his own greatness, telling those present that God had given him power to warn the archbishop and others. But they did not take his warnings seriously and now, therefore, God would punish them for their disobedience. When the punishment came to Janani Luwum it was swift and violent. According.to our source, Amin pulled out his pistol and shot the archbishop several times in the chest. He died at once and his body was secretly disposed of, possibly dumped into Lake.Victoria along with others.

Bishop Kivingere remembers the last time Janani Luwum spoke to his bishops, leading them in their devotions on the day of his death. He appeared to them as one "full of the Lord" and spoke to them of Jesus on the mountain alone, praying, when he saw his disciples on a journey, "making headway painfully." Janani remarked that in the last two or three days the Lord had seen an archbishop making headway painfully. "But I see the road very clear. . . ." The road was the road of discipleship, the road which the Lord had traveled before. It was the road of justice and truth.

In Janani Luwum we have seen the Church Catholic embodied, the bishop leading the church, the focus of its unity and integrity. This does not mean that he was a pompous, obviously powerful figure. He was not. And yet the power was there. As Bishop Kivingere has pointed out, he was "full of the Lord." And the church which he led possessed the essentials of Scripture, creeds, sacraments and episcopal ministry, but it possessed them in a creative and life-giving manner. The church which the archbishop led was not bound to past customs, as is apparent when we take into account the variety of lay ministries which are so vital to that church and provide for so much of its enthusiasm to witness.

In the archbishop we see one who by his courageous life and heroic death recalls the church everywhere to its essential being in Christ. Gothic cathedrals, smooth-running parishes, good looking clergy—all pale in the light of Janani's death, which illumines the death of the Lord, now risen to make all things new. Nonessentials can have value, but only in relation to that which is essential. In order to remember this the church must constantly be reformed and its people renewed.

Janani Luwum loved his country and it was partly because of that love that he spoke out against the evils which were destroying it. He could have acquiesced to pressure and become the government's pawn, but he did not. He kept his distance from an evil government and did not cease his efforts to transform its president, recalling him to his true being in God. Therefore he, with his bishops, advised Amin to "let the law replace the gun"—only thus could the good and true image of the nation be restored.

Finally, Janani Luwum not only understood Christ's mission, he was that mission, representing Christ to the world. The Christ revealed in Janani's martyrdom stands for justice and truth, for renewal and reform, empowering his followers with grace and mercy to be his body in the world.

Notes

---

1. Quoted from a typed manuscript entitled, "Report of a very serious incident at the Archbishop's House in the early hours of Saturday, 5th February 1977," p. 1.

2. Quoted from a typed manuscript entitled, "A Prepared Response of the House of Bishops of the C.O.U.-Rwanda-Burundi and Boga Zaire to his Excellency on Wednesday 16th February 1977, at the Conference Centre in Kampala," pp. 1–2.

3. For this account I am dependent upon the eye witness report by Bishop Kivingere provided to me on tape by the Rev. George Woodard of Trinity Church, New York City.

4. The source for this account by the archbishop's former driver is Joseph Adero Ngala reporting from the Tanzania-Uganda border for the *National Catholic Reporter*, March 25, 1977, p. 5. The report was corroborated in its main point by Henry Kyemba, former Ugandan Minister of Health: *New York Times*, June 6, 1977. See also, *Newsweek*, February 28, 1977, p. 35; and *Time*, March 7, 1977, pp. 19–29.

· 4 ·

Understanding the Faith
of the Church

- Have you ever felt completely, utterly alone in the world
  with no point of human—or any other—contact? What
  helped you "get out of" this mood?
- Have you ever seen a potentially depressing week stretch
  before you and made it bearable by remembering something good that was to happen at the end of it?
- Do you believe in heaven? Hell?
- If you were to write your own eulogy, what sorts of
  things would you say about yourself as of right now?

The tone of these questions is not meant to be a clue to or
warning about the contents of *Understanding the Faith of the Church*,
although they are all questions that could be answered, at least
in part, by reading the selections from the book which follow.
Actually, this volume in The Church's Teaching Series is one of
the most hopeful and rewarding books you could hope to find. It
is about the greatest adventure one could have—the adventure
of the search for an understanding of the nature of God, God as
a father, God as Holy Spirit, and God in Christ. This is a book,
on the other hand, dealing with matters of life and death importance—literally. This book is a far cry from an ancient
leather-bound theology tome. It is an exciting book because it
asks all the hard questions about the fate of the human race, as
well as the easy ones.

The first selection is called "The Search for an 'Other.'" It
examines the age-old search of humans for an "other," a force
both "other" and outside and beyond themselves and their

human weaknesses—and yet a force that is personal and "real," not an abstraction. Christians know that "other" as God made known to us through Jesus Christ. But there are degrees of knowing and of belief, and this will be a challenging reading for anyone at any stage of spiritual development and doctrinal belief.

The second selection is a whole chapter from the book, titled from the Creed we have all probably said a thousand times and not thought about as often as we should have: ". . . and the Life of the World to Come." This selection deals with vital issues for all Christians because it deals with those issues that are peculiarly part of the Christian religion. Christians, to be Christians, must deal with the most difficult of all belief areas—*hope*. And hope for people who are also able to see the reasons for being without hope in the world around them is very precarious and hard come by. For Christians hope and belief in the world to come is not a pretty thought to trot out on holidays. It is a tenet of faith and one of the most difficult. There is something in our nature that makes it much easier to accept gracefully and resignedly the blows that seem to be our lot. But that is much too easy.

The Use Guide that was prepared for *Understanding the Faith of the Church* contains a discussion question that might be helpful after a reading of the final selection. "What has God already done that can make us confident of what he will do?"

Human Identity
and the Question of God

The Search for an "Other"

Where, then, is a real "other" to be found? People look, as a matter of fact, in a variety of places for an "other" to which they can answer. Some seem to find it in abstractions like "humanity" or "the welfare of society." Others find it in the customs of a particular society, which do indeed, at times, seem to speak—to make demands, and in doing so to shape the lineaments of my identity as a human person. Others again find a significant "other" in some cause in which they can be swept up and through which they can be drawn out of themselves into creative action.

The truth is, however, that none of these can be any more than a substitute, and a temporary one at that, for a significant "other." All of them, in the last resort, are creatures of the very people who turn to them·in need. Whether one thinks of the institutions of a given society, or the ideals and hopes which are wrapped up in a particular cause, one realizes in the end that they are products of human creativity and human aspiration. They cannot really answer people back. They cannot take an initiative with people. They can only do and be what people enable them to do and be. None of them, therefore, can qualify as a true "other" for the persons involved with them.

55

The Transcendent "Other"

Our question still stands, then. Where are we to find the "other" which answers to modern humanity? Where is the "other" which corresponds to a humanity which is forever transcending its world and its own works? To put the question the other way around, to whom do I respond as I make myself and my world? This is the modern form of the question of God. It is the question of a real and transcendent "other" which is the point of reference, the Speaker and the Word, for humankind's self-discovery.

Why do we say, though, that this question about an "other" is a form of the question of God? We say so first of all because it is a question about something which genuinely transcends humanity, something which is not under our control or capable of being shaped by us. It is a question about that which goes beyond humanity in such a way as to be the continuing partner of a humanity which is constantly transcending itself. In the language of traditional theology, it is a question about an "other" which is independent in its own infinite being.

Second, this is the question of God because it concerns something which, while transcendent, is also present with humanity in the most intimate possible way. *God* is not properly the same of an abstraction or an absent absolute. It is a word for a transcendent "other" which gives itself in the most intimate and deep-reaching dialogue with humankind. *God* means not just a transcendence, but a transcendence which speaks.

Third, it is the question of God because it is a question about an "other" which is not only transcendent and present, but also *ultimate*. Self-transcending humanity cannot discover itself and its identity in a dialogue with an "other" which is less than truly final. To put this same thing another way, the meaning of human existence does not appear in any particular historical "jelling" of its identity. It consists in a relationship with God, who pulls it beyond every historical realization of its identity.

Fourth, it is the question of God because the "other"

which is asked about it is a *universal* "other." This "other" does not belong to the private moments of life alone, but speaks through the larger world of things and people which the enclaves of privacy exclude. It is the "other" which allows the world to have a proper and independent reality of its own, and, at the same time, to be a vehicle for people's encounter with the divine.

It must be clear, however, that the question of God is not answered, but merely raised, in this way. The question calls for such an "other," but unless a relationship with it is given to us, the question remains unanswered. Our situation is rather like that of children abandoned by their parents at birth. They can feel the reality of their parents' absence, they can point to their need of them now, they can even infer what they must have been like. None of this, though, will provide them with a loving embrace, a face turned towards them, or the sound of a parent's voice.

All questions about God, then, come to focus on one question: *Has God revealed himself to us?* The Christian theologian maintains that the ultimate questions of human life can be answered only in the self-revelation of God. If God has appeared to humankind in revelation, establishing a relationship with us, then our questions about identity and the meaning of human life are answered in principle. If God continues to appear to us, maintaining his relationship with us, the questions can be answered in our own lives.

"... and the Life of the World to Come"

In Christian faith there is a built-in orientation to the future. It has been there from the beginning. Jesus proclaimed that God's Kingdom was at hand and that its powers were at work even in the present. In this way he created expectancy. He pointed people ahead to a future in which the promise of their present, the promise which Jesus himself represented, would be fulfilled. Furthermore, Jesus' disciples understood his Resurrection to be the beginning of that fulfillment. When God raised Jesus from the dead, they insisted, he opened the door leading to that New Age for which the faithful had always hoped. They were certain, therefore, that their own time was the era of the inauguration of God's Rule, of "the world to come"; and that they could, for that reason, look confidently forward to its complete actualization. Saint Paul even describes the gift of the Holy Spirit as a "down payment" or "first installment" which assures that "what is mortal" will be "swallowed up by life" (1 Cor. 5:4–5).

Thus Christian life is governed not only by faith and love, but also by hope: that is, by a confident expectation that God will bring to fulfillment the promise contained in people's present life in Christ. An essential aspect of the relationship with God which the creeds portray is, therefore, this: that when we stand in that relationship, we are stretched out in hope toward "the resurrection of the dead and the life of the world to come."

The full meaning of this Christian hopefulness, however, is not easy to grasp. One might choose to understand it as just an instance or illustration of the fact that all human existence is directed toward the future—as indeed it is. The poet's saying, "Hope springs eternal," does not apply only to Christians. It describes everyone. All of us are compelled to look ahead to the "not yet" and to depend upon it. This is not only because we want the future to provide what the present and past have denied us. It is also because only the future can guarantee our secure possession of what the past and the present have already given us. Until tomorrow, all is uncertain.

The meaning of Christian hope, however, is not exhausted in this commonplace dependence on the future. Far from it. Christian hope is rooted in present reality—in the fact of God's self-giving in Christ and the Holy Spirit. For that reason it goes beyond wishing or wanting. It becomes a kind of expecting. "The life of the world to come" is not a dream or an ideal to be realized. It is a reality which God is even now creating in Christ; and that fact makes Christian hoping distinctive in its quality.

To say this, however, does not make such hope any easier to understand. In the course of the church's history, it has expressed itself in a number of different ways; and some of these seem difficult to justify or to make sense of. Every now and then, for example, a movement appears which announces "the end of the world"; and we ask ourselves whether this indeed is the sole content of Christian hope for the human world. Or again, as many critics of Christianity have pointed out, this hope sometimes takes a form which encourages people to care nothing for the problems of the here and now because they are taught to look for "pie in the sky by and by." But if things of this sort do not represent full or authentic Christian hoping, what does?

So there are many questions to ask about "the life of the world to come." In the first place, we want to know what the content of that hope is. In the second place, we want to know what effect Christian hoping has on the character of Christian life here and now. What does it mean to lead a life formed by this hope in God's "new thing"? These are the questions which this chapter will address.

Heaven and Hell

Before we can set about this task directly, however, there is a preliminary job to be done. There is a popular version of Christian hope which is current among churchgoers and non-churchgoers alike. It is familiar, in one form or another, to almost everyone, and it provides the framework within which most people understand phrases like "the life of the world to come." In fact, however, it distorts the meaning of biblical and creedal teaching about human destiny. By looking critically at this understanding of Christian hope, therefore, we can hope to get some of the issues straight and even begin to see something of the true sense of New Testament language about human destiny.

In fact this popular version of Christian hope does not often use the classical language of Christian teaching. It does not talk much about the life of the world to come or the Kingdom of God or resurrection. Its central symbols are the words *heaven* and *hell,* and the context in which they are used is that of belief in the survival, or "immortality," of the human soul. Heaven is understood to be a place or a state of being in which people are forever happy and blessed—in which things are "right." Men and women go to heaven after their deaths on certain conditions. If they have believed the Gospel and kept God's commandments, they will be sent to this place of happiness when they die. If on the contrary they are disobedient, they run the risk of torment, of punishment in hell, which is also pictured as a present and available "place" or "state."

For centuries this set of ideas and images has been central for people's picture of their ultimate future. It has represented all that they have known or understood of Christian hope. Today, perhaps, the situation is somewhat different.

There are few persons now who thoroughly accept this understanding of their situation. Many have doubts about, say, hell, or about the survival of the soul. Many reject the whole picture outright. Even the latter, however, are convinced that this scheme gives a true account of the Christian hope. Yet it takes only a brief look at the Scriptures, and especially the New Testament, to see that this picture of things distorts the thrust of their witness.

Consider first of all the idea of survival, of what we nowadays call "immortality." The New Testament only infrequently uses the term *immortality*, and its primary affirmation is that immortality, properly speaking, belongs only to God (1 Tim. 6:16, 1:17). When immortality is ascribed to human beings (1 Cor. 15:53, 54), therefore, it appears not as a natural possession, but as a gift from God. Immortality in fact is used to talk, not about survival, but about the quality of life in the New Age. It is a gift of the Holy Spirit in the resurrection, not something that people have in their own right.

Our popular version of Christian hope, therefore, gets the Scriptures' conception of immortality slightly askew. It uses it not to describe the glory of a human life shared with God in the Kingdom, but more or less neutrally, to speak of the automatic persistence of the human self beyond the grave. Yet on the latter subject, the Scriptures are strangely silent. The Old Testament knows nothing of an automatic "life after death"—except, of course, the shadow existence of *Sheol*, which hardly qualifies as life. And if the New Testament speaks of life after death, it is always a matter of a life shared with Jesus—that is, a *new* life conferred by God's gift, and not an automatic possession (Lk. 23:43, 2 Cor. 4:10–11, 5:8). To be immortal is to share through Jesus in the life of the Coming Age.

Then, in the second place, consider the idea of heaven as it is used in this popular version of Christian hope. One of the phrases which the New Testament uses to refer to the future which God has inaugurated in Christ is *Kingdom of Heaven*. Saint Matthew uses it, as we have seen, to mean the same thing as *Kingdom of God* because, for reasons of reverence, he does not wish to refer directly to God. It was easy enough, however, for later readers of his Gospel to think that he was talking, not about the Rule of God, but about "the realm of heaven" or "the celestial realm." This misunderstanding was encouraged by two other factors. One of these was the biblical imagery which portrays "heaven" or "the heavens" as the place from which God and the Messiah and his angels would come to consummate the New Age. Another factor was the belief, encouraged by a long tradition of pagan philosophy and religion, in a separate, heavenly "world" of the gods. The writers of the New Testament, however, did not think of this celestial realm as identical with, or as a substitute for, the Age to Come; and it is this identification which makes, or starts, the trouble, by turning heaven into an alternative or parallel world where things are better than they are in this one.

And finally, what about the picture of hell in this popular version of Christian hope? People often go to the pages of the New Testament to "prove" the reality of hell. What one finds there, though, is not a concept of hell in the modern sense, but a conviction that the coming of God's Rule is a moment of judgment for all the forces that oppose it. When the New Age appears, as indeed it began to appear in the ministry of Jesus, those who reject it shall find the reward which accords with their choice. That is what the New Testament, and the apocalyptic tradition on which it draws at this point, firmly believes. When God acts to put things right, they will be put right; and if that means the rejection of some people because they have finally and irrevocably rejected God, then so it must be.

In primitive Christianity, to be sure, this rejection of the wicked was pictured in several alternative ways. Some held that the wicked would simply be left to death—forgotten because destroyed. Others held that the wicked would be raised from the dead for eternal punishment. Still others, while they agreed that the wicked would be raised from the dead and punished, were sure that this punishment would be therapeutic and educational—that in the end all would be brought into God's Kingdom. No matter which of these views one held, however, hell was not conceived of as a permanent "world" in itself, permanently available for occupancy. It was a product or an aspect of the action in which God did final right—in which he consummated the New Age; and the emphasis was not on punishment, but on God's desire, indeed his solemn purpose, to consummate the good thing which he had done in Christ.

Problems in the Popular Version of Christian Hope

Let us turn, however, from the imagery of this popular version of Christian hope—from the ideas of immortality, heaven, and hell as it conceives them—and look at the meaning of the over-all picture of human destiny which they are used to convey. Here too we see serious distortion of the sense of Christian hoping.

Notice first of all that this popular scheme offers very little hope and breeds very little hopefulness. Jesus came calling for repentance because the Kingdom of God, the promised New Age, was at hand. Thus his message was indeed one of hope. It proclaimed that the promises of God through the prophets were already being fulfilled—that the blind were receiving their sight and the poor hearing good news. What though is the message of our popular version of Christian hope? Heaven is not a good thing coming, least of all a good thing which has appeared in our midst. On the contrary, it is a good thing waiting for us to win it; and the usefulness of achieving it is underscored by the fact that the only alternative is hell. Consequently, it is not very frequently "eager longing" (Rom. 8:19) which inspires people when they think of heaven. It is just as likely to be a sense of having a task to perform in order to avoid torment or in order to prove oneself. And that is not hopefulness.

This, however, is not the only problem with this version of Christian belief in the future. There is also the fact that it concentrates wholly on the fate of the individual. So used are we to thinking in individualistic terms, that we hardly notice the difference between the image of heaven as popularly conceived and that of the Kingdom of God or the World to Come. These, when you stop to consider them, turn out to be images of a *world transformed*. They point to the prospect that the purpose of God's creation shall be realized: that the whole human world, in all its variety, shall enter upon a new age by truly becoming *God's* world. This prospect certainly involves and affects individuals, but it does not come about merely through individual choice or private goodness. Consequently, any version of Christian hope which centers only on the question, *What becomes of me?*, is one which falsifies both the New Testament and the creeds. True Christian hope has social and indeed cosmic dimensions. It answers the question, *What becomes of us?*

Further, as we have seen, this popular version of Christian hope seems to understand heaven as another world alongside this one—a world which is coexistent with ours and parallels it, but nevertheless remains separate from it. That is what appears to be implied by such expressions as "this world" or "the world beyond" or "going to heaven." The idea is, presumably, that under certain circumstances one can leave "here" and go "there." Philosophers have often criticized this picture, arguing that what it adds up to is a devaluation of human life here in this world. Christians are said to teach that it is the heavenly world alone which is ultimately real and worth caring about. They are accused, therefore, of regarding this world as a "vale of tears," in which wrong must simply be endured for the sake of earning heaven.

Such a duality of worlds, however, is no part of what is truly meant by hope in "the life of the world to come." On the contrary, "the world to come" is this world—but transformed, altered, and renewed. To use the language of popular belief, heaven is not "another" world at all. It is our present life re-formed according to God's will. What God is organizing in this world through the ministry, death, and Resurrection of Jesus is its redemption, not its evacuation.

And that, we must finally add, is the whole point of the idea of "the resurrection of the dead," which the creeds mention in close conjunction with "the life of the world to come." The popular version, as we are calling it, of Christian hope has a hard time making sense of this idea of resurrection. Just as, in the particular case of Jesus, we moderns will take resurrection to mean mere resuscitation of a dead organism, so in the face of the idea of the "general resurrection" we tend to conceive it (if we think about it at all) as a matter of an individual's body coming suddenly back to life and getting reattached to its soul, now located in heaven (or perhaps in hell).

This misses the whole point of the New Testament idea of resurrection. Resurrection is the beginning of the New Age. It is the event through which those who have died have the new life in God made real for them. The term *resurrection*, therefore, does not refer to the bringing of corpses back to life—and for two good reasons. In the first place, the life to which those who are awakened from death are raised is a new, transformed life. It is not the old sort of life in the old sort of context. Resurrection does not bring people *back* to anything. It takes them into a new context of living, a world in which all things are summed up in Christ (Eph. 1:10). In the second place, that word *body* in the phrase "resurrection of the body" can be misleading to people who do not talk in the way Saint Paul did. The phrase is his; and since he distinguishes body very carefully from "flesh and blood" (1 Cor. 15:50) which is "perishable," we can be sure that "resurrection of the body" does not mean bringing corpses back to life. Most interpreters think that *body*, when used in this connection, means, for Paul, the individual person as a whole, taken apart from any distinction between flesh and soul. My body is simply myself as I am real for others in my world. To speak of resurrection of the body, therefore, is to speak of the re-bodying of the human person in the context of the new life of Christ.

What we have to say in the end, therefore, is something like this. The world as we now know and experience it is a world in which death comes as the final word spoken to everyone and everything; and death cuts people off in an absolute way. When one speaks of resurrection, however, one is speaking of this same human world so transformed and renewed that the final word is *life in God. Resurrection*, in other words, has two dimensions of meaning which people normally miss. First of all, it stands for something which happens in and for a whole world, a whole context of life, and not just for individuals. Second, it is a symbol which means not so much revival, as it does renewal and transformation. Resurrection is the transfer of our individual and common lives in all their dimensions and relations to a new level of existence "in Christ."

Hope in the God Who Raised Jesus

In the light of this long and critical look at the popular version of Christian hope, it ought to be possible to return to our original question about the content of Christian hope. This question itself, however, has two parts, and they need to be kept distinct from each other for purposes of theological discussion. The content of Christian hope includes both what Christians hope *in* and what they hope *for*; and these are, at least in part, different.

Christian hoping is like Christian believing. That is, it is directed to God. Whatever it is that Christians hope for, the reason why they can hope at all is that they know God has given them a basis for their hope by raising Jesus from the dead and by involving them with his new life. Thus the answer to the question, "In what do Christians hope?" is the simplest answer possible. "They hope in God." Jesus reveals God to be the one who does right and who gives himself in love to be with his people. He also reveals God to be the one who can bring good out of evil and life out of death. And that is why Christians live hopefully—not as naive optimists about human goodness or human intentions, but as people who have learned that God's love has transforming power and that it can be trusted.

And maybe this is the point at which the essential difference between true Christian hoping and that popular version of Christian hope which we have just examined becomes clear. For if it is true that the "getting to heaven" syndrome really does not involve much hopefulness at all, the reason is that it sees God merely as the operator of a cosmic reward-and-punishment system. It has never grasped the fact that God, as seen in the Gospel which Jesus and his apostles preached, is at work in the world to fulfill the purpose of his creation, which means to bring about the good thing which his act of creation has intended from the beginning. That good thing, which we have learned to call "the Kingdom of God" and "the life of the world to come," is not, therefore, just a given and available reality which people have to possess for themselves by playing the game according to the rules. No, it is something which God is up to in Christ—something which he is already bringing about in them, through them, and with them. That is the reason why they can hope; and that is the reason why their hope is centered on God. They do not hope in themselves, or in any objective system of rewards and punishments. They hope in the God who brought the children of Israel out of bondage and who raised Jesus from the dead.

Hope for This World

But if God is the one *in whom* Christians hope, what is it *for which* they hope?

From one point of view, that question is easy enough to answer. People who hope in God take delight in God and trust God. Consequently, what they hope for is simply the fulfillment of his purposes and of their relationship with him. To say the same thing in another way, the object of their hope is the full realization of the life in Christ; for that defines both God's purposes for humanity and humanity's proper relationship to God.

In other words, the content of Christian hope, that to which Christians look forward, is the perfection of something which is already real in Christ and of which they already have a taste through the gift of the Holy Spirit.

It is important, moreover, to say this and to say it emphatically. Often the imagery of Christian hope gives, falsely, the impression that what the church hopes for is something which is absolutely "not of this world," something of which no one has ever heard or dreamt, much less experienced. It is understandable, moreover, how this impression could be given. The rhetoric of Christian hoping is high and enthusiastic, to say the least. It pictures a world of "endless sabbaths" and "golden slippers"—a new Jerusalem come down out of heaven, "its radiance like a most rare jewel, like a jasper, clear as crystal" (Rev. 21:11). Such language is hardly likely to make people think it is referring to hard, salty reality.

On the other hand, this rhetoric must be taken as more than a way of tossing up idle, and ultimately meaningless, images of happiness. In the first place, all of these images grow directly out of the realities of human life as we know it. They point to good things in human life of whose goodness we are intensely aware from time to time. To describe the Kingdom of God as a feast is to remember the joys of a solemnly happy party with good friends. To describe the world to come as a new Jerusalem is to acknowledge the grandeur and splendor of the life of a great city, a city at whose center is the presence of the Holy One. To speak of endless sabbaths and golden slippers is to recall the deep refreshment of contemplative rest, and the sense of fulfillment which sometimes occurs when people "dress up" for a special occasion or event. These images may sound fantastic; but in fact they all grow out of real experience.

But there is more to say than just this. For what these images are trying to describe—and not just the terms in which they describe it—is itself a part of experience and of the real world. To hope for the Kingdom of God is not to hope for a never-never land. It is to hope for the fulfillment of what people have already begun to know and experience in Christ. The imagery of Christian hoping is calculated to suggest not that believers' minds are focused on some dream, but that they hardly know how to express their wonder at the prospect of the full actualization of something which, in its bare beginnings, is already with them. What these images convey, in other words, is the idea of a final enhancement, fulfillment, or realization of a good which has already entered into the present order of things. "World to come" is the name of this world when its affairs are put right and it "graduates," so to speak, to a new form of relationship to God. It is not the name of a substitute world of a quite different sort.

Hope for a World Transformed

Yet clearly enough the life of the world to come is no mere reproduction of the present state of affairs; and this side of the picture must be emphasized as well. It is true that "world to come" refers to the world of God's original creation. At the same time, however, it pictures that world as existing and being experienced on a higher plane. Saint Paul, as we have seen, insists that "flesh and blood cannot inherit the kingdom of God" (1 Cor. 15:50). By the same token he implies that to share in the Resurrection involves making a transition through death from one level of existence to a new one.

So it is with the resurrection of the dead. What is sown is perishable, what is raised is imperishable. It is sown in dishonor, it is raised in glory. It is sown in weakness, it is raised in power. It is sown a physical body, it is raised a spiritual body (1 Cor. 15:42–44).

In other words, the life of the world to come really does involve a change in the way things are. The change is so profound that it involves a kind of dying and rebirth, whose end product is the same people, making up the same world, but people whose life is led in an entirely different mode, a revised relationship to God. It is as though human existence, like an old melody, were to be transposed into a new key. There is continuity between the two—real continuity; but there is also real discontinuity.

And these two truths must be held in balance in any account of Christian hoping. Throughout the New Testament, and indeed throughout Christian history, there runs a contrast between a tendency to see the New Age as utterly different from the present and a tendency to emphasize its continuity with experience and life here and now. It is the latter tendency, for example, which surfaces when, in the Gospels, emphasis is laid on the bodily, physical reality of the risen Christ and his recognizability. The point of that emphasis is to insist that the Jesus of the New Creation is the same person with whom the disciples walked and talked in Galilee. On the other hand, these same Gospels insist also that the risen Christ is a mysterious and awesome figure, one who very obviously does not belong to the present order of things, but one who comes to it bearing its future. In this way the Gospels call attention to what we have called the discontinuity between old and new, then and now.

This tension, which must be present in any honest account of Christian hoping, is embodied in the important but unfashionable word *supernatural*. That word has, at least recently, been almost universally misused and misunderstood. In popular speech its meaning has been degraded. It is thought to refer to the magical or the "spooky" or the merely miraculous. In academic circles, on the other hand, it is employed as a shorthand way of referring to that "other world," the heavenly parallel of this, which it is believed that Christian faith affirms. Talk of the supernatural, therefore, is naturally condemned either as sheer superstition or as a kind of dualism; that is, a division of reality into inferior and superior worlds.

In fact, however, the term *supernatural* has a perfectly proper meaning. Correctly understood, it means human life as we have it (that is, the "natural") enhanced and taken beyond itself through a perfected relationship with God. And that precisely defines the nature of Christian hope. Such hope does not focus on another world, but on this world. On the other hand, it sees this world surpassing anything that it has ever been before through participation in the life of the risen Christ—life in a "new key." You might say that Christian hoping amounts to a settled confidence that God is completing his work of bringing people to share Jesus' new life, "the life of the world to come," the resurrected life. And that is precisely a *super*natural, but not an *un*natural, goal.

That is why all efforts to picture "what it will be like" must fail. All that human language can do when it tries to grasp "the life of the world to come" is to extrapolate in various ways. It can talk of *final* victory over the things which cut people off from God and their neighbor—i.e., death and sin. It can try to imagine what this might be like by using terms such as "light" and "immortality" and "the vision of God." Nevertheless there are limits to the usefulness of such language. The supernatural can only be pointed to; it cannot be described. What happens when people truly share the life of God in love cannot be said except figuratively; and the most important figure for us is not one of our own images, but the person of Jesus himself. He is the one whose human living and dying, in their moral quality, embody the presence of God for us, and so reach out and touch "the life of the world to come."

Life Shaped by Hope

Even though it is impossible to describe "the life of the world to come" in any save indirect terms, it is by no means impossible to say how hoping in God affects human existence here and now. For hope does make a difference. It is an essential factor in the life of a community of forgiven sinners.

In the first place, hope makes a difference because it rescues people from the abyss of despair and cynicism on the one hand, and from the cloud lands of naive optimism on the other. The Christian believer is not the sort of uncritical idealist who has to hide from the realities of human perversity and meanness behind a mist of illusion. Neither is the believer the sort of person who, when illusion is dispelled, becomes embittered, disappointed, and hopeless. Trusting in God and in the power of God's love, such a person has no need to be deceived about things as they are. It is not necessary to believe that everything is really all right; or, having discovered that it is not, to think the exact contrary—that everything is all wrong. Christians can perceive the imperfection and willful wrongness which infects not just the world but even themselves, and yet know that God works with people and in them and that his grace will ultimately triumph. Christian hope is not optimism; it is trust in God.

There is, however, still another way in which Christian hoping makes a difference for the way people think and live. In a profound and permanent way, it affects the manner in which they understand and face the fact of death—both their own death and that of others.

There is, of course, a terror which is occasioned by dying itself, as distinct from death. In these days, more often than in the past, dying is a protracted process. It involves increasing illness, helplessness, pain, and, above all, a sense of uselessness and isolation. To persons in these circumstances the Gospel offers genuine, though not easy, assurance. It is not the assurance that they will always or necessarily get well or get better. It is, rather, the assurance that their dying is not without meaning. Self-surrender through silent and patient self-giving was the way in which God made himself present for us in Christ. It is also, if Saint Paul is right about the manner in which the new life is born, a way in which people like us can find God. Dying, with all the trouble it inevitably brings upon people's spirits, can in Christ be a pointer to life, the embodiment of hope for new life.

The ultimate terror, however, does not lie in the process of dying. It lies in death itself. For death is rightly and instinctively perceived, not just as the disintegration of an organism, but as the violation of a positive moral good. It is the final cutting off of the self from all that it loves and from all that has given it life. It is true that for many people death is the end of a great deal of pain and trouble. Strangely, though, it is the rare person who sees death, when actually facing it, as relief. Most people fear death, or at least reject it; and the reason for this is not just their fear of ceasing to be. Rather, the reason is that they do not want to be separated either from the other human beings or from the God with whom they have shared themselves and in whom they have discovered themselves. Death is the end of loving and being loved. That is why it means extinction and why it is supremely hated and feared.

Christian faith, however, is based on a story which tells of love's triumph over sin and death—over the two things in this world that have seemed irrevocably to cut people off from the "other." Christian faith affirms, on the basis of Jesus' Resurrection, that death cannot finally "disconnect" the life with which God shares himself in love: that, in fact, death is one step on the way to the fulfillment of life in the New Creation. In this way Christian faith helps people to hope in the midst of death. It enables them to face death with a sense both that it means something positive in human experience, and that it does not bring the world to an end. The world's end, in Christian faith, is not its finish for me in death, but its renewal in the world to come.

Finally, though, hope makes a difference in the way people live and act here and now. Those who, through faith, have caught a glimpse of the love of God as it touches them in Christ, and who therefore hope for the Kingdom of God, become understandably impatient with the present state of human affairs. Hoping, for them, becomes a kind of reaching out for the future God is bringing. It translates itself into efforts to make the world in which we presently live look, if only a little bit, like the New Creation which God is bringing.

There are two very good reasons why hope has this effect. In the first place, hope which focuses on a real prospect of good is bound to make people critical of whatever in their present situation falls short of that for which they hope. Hopeless people are always passive. They do not see how things can be much better than they are; so they cannot be persuaded to stir themselves to try to improve them. Hopeful people, however, are a different breed. They see the present state of affairs in the light of the things for which they hope, and they set about trying to make those good things real even here and now.

In the second place, hope which is genuine fills people with joy, in the same way that the prospect of Christmas fills small children with joy. And in their joy they begin to rehearse the good thing which is coming—to run through it in their minds and to act it out in reality. They begin to behave as though it were already here, out of sheer pleasure.

Christian history is full of such dress rehearsals for the Kingdom of God. In a way, all Christian worship, all enacting of the church's liturgy, is just such an affair, an attempt to actualize in the present moment, through words and music and ritual dance, the beauty and the goodness of the new creation in Christ. In quite another way, but in line with the same logic, such a movement as monasticism attempts to find a social form within which to actualize, and so symbolize for the world, certain dimensions of "the life of the world to come." The same can be said of many other phenomena in the life of the church, from its perpetual singing of hymns to its perpetual fostering of political and social reform in the world. The church is a community which is getting itself and its world ready for the life of the world to come, even while others see, on every hand, only the prospect of death.

Thus, hope throws people into action in the effort to conform the world now to its future in Christ. This indeed is one way of understanding the whole realm of what is studied in Christian ethics as well as in the theological sciences of the interior life. Think, on the one hand, of an individual act of kindness, or of the attempt of a group of people to achieve social justice for others, or of public acts of philanthropy. Then think, on the other hand, of the practice of spirituality—the cultivation of habits of prayer and meditation and interior collectedness before God. Both of these kinds of activity can be seen as expressions of hope—as attempts to actualize in the present, if only in a partial way, the glory of what will be in "the life of the age to come."

Conclusion

It is important not to forget, however, that these forms of Christian action really are expressions of *hope*. The people who engage in them are people who live as forgiven sinners in a world which in fact is not conformed to its supernatural future. Their own hoping, and the action to which it gives rise, may well be touched by the very evil it seeks to overcome. That is why, in the end, the creeds present us with a declaration not of present fulfillment, but precisely of future hope. Even when our attempts to live up to the Kingdom fall short of perfection, even when we know that after all the future which God is bringing cannot be fully experienced here and now, it is still possible to trust God in the power of the Holy Spirit on the basis of his work in Christ, and to say, "We look for the resurrection of the dead and the life of the world to come."

· 5 ·

Liturgy for Living

- Have you ever experienced a change in your life that was so deep and far-reaching you would call it a *transformation*, an actual rebirth or redirectioning?
- Did you ever have the experience of going into your parish church for a service in a state of depression or despondency and coming out to see a new world? How did this happen?
- Are you aware of the rituals you create in your ordinary, everyday routines—rituals relating to dressing and getting ready to go to work in the morning, rituals relating to going to bed at night? Have you ever thought about what these rituals might mean beyond what they seem to mean outwardly? Could it be that you brush your teeth the way your father used to brush his? Could it be that you think about people you have loved who are no longer with you before you go to sleep?

You will find in your reading of selections from *Liturgy for Living* that liturgy once referred, quite simply, to the daily lives of people. Christian liturgy, grounded totally as it is in the life of Christ, is a great transformation. Because Christ was unlike any other, so the liturgy of his life is unlike any other.

Liturgy for Living is about what it promises. It traces the origins of liturgy as it is known to Anglicans all over the world and to other Christians in the universal Catholic tradition. It focuses in on the Book of Common Prayer, dealing with the various offices, services, and other liturgies. The volume never deals in surface generalities. The attempt is always to explain the surface and then to dig beneath it.

The first selection from *Liturgy for Living* is called "Implications and Consequences of Liturgy." It is a profound examination of "why"—why liturgy is important to Christians and, by implication, to God. The selection is grounded in the belief that the fulfilled life for Christians is found when their lives in and out of the church are interwoven. As the text says: ". . . liturgy not only has consequences for life. Life has consequences for the liturgy."

The second selection is called "Living the Liturgy" and it is specifically about the vigorous pursuit of the liturgical life *now*, at this moment in the twentieth century. It makes a strong case for the use of the forms of worship outlined in the new Prayer Book.

It would be hoped that people reading the selections from *Liturgy for Living* would try to re-evaluate their liturgical lives as a result of the reading. For we all do have liturgical lives in or out of church and being "in touch" with and aware of the liturgical part of our lives cannot help but be an important and enriching experience. One of the great gifts of Christianity has been the richness and totality of its liturgy and its inherent belief that all that is human is potentially good and worthy of being lifted up.

Implications and
Consequences of Liturgy

The fact that Christian liturgy is related so closely to Christ himself on the one hand and to the daily lives of Christians on the other bears further examination. It is the purpose of this chapter to trace some of the implications and consequences of liturgy.

Christian Worship
as the Transformation of Time

In the last chapter we found ourselves saying three rather different things. On the one hand we found that Christ fulfills and pre-empts each of the aspects of worship we discussed. He is the sacrifice, the priest, the prayer, the myth, and the ritual. In short *he* is our liturgy. At the same time our lives as Christians, lived obediently to the covenant of trust and obedience, also constitute sacrifice, priesthood, prayer, myth, and ritual. *We* are the Christian liturgy. Furthermore, the gatherings of the Christian community to worship the God revealed in Christ are characterized by liturgy, sacrifice, prayer, and ritual, led by officiants called priests. How can Christian worship mean all these things simultaneously?

A clue to this complicated situation is to be found in what we have already said in Chapter 3 about the role of the Holy

Spirit in worship. We said that the Spirit constitutes the unity between the holy God and the finite, particular manifestations of the divine. Jesus Christ and the Father are one "in the unity of the Holy Spirit" as numerous Prayer Book collects express it. The Spirit is the bond of unity—not only between these two ways God has of being God, but also between Christ Jesus, who lived and died in Palestine nearly two thousand years ago, and our lives and our worship "at all times and in all places" and especially here and now. We are one with him in the Spirit, our liturgy one with his, our sacrifice one with his, our prayer one with his. This unity is accomplished by a transformation of time.

In the act of worship, we come into the presence of God. In the ecstasy of prayer, our spirits are caught up in God's Spirit. Since God is equally present at all times and in all places in the Spirit, our time in particular is contemporary with that time in which the decisive revelation of God appeared.

> Were you there when they crucified my Lord? . . .
> Were you there when they nailed him to the tree? . . .
> Were you there when they laid him in the tomb?[1]

The answer implied is yes! And we were there also when God raised him from the dead, and when he sat at God's right hand.

When myth becomes history, that history, whether of the exodus or of the cross and resurrection, has the possibility of entering subsequent moments of history, to transform them. "Not with our fathers did the Lord make this covenant, but with us, who are all of us here alive this day" (Dt. 5:3). Those words were said to the people of the Old Covenant, gathered to renew the covenant many generations after that covenant was first made on Mount Sinai. The book of Deuteronomy, in which the verse appears, has been dated as early as the eighth century B.C. and as late as the fifth, but in any case centuries after the exodus and the initiating of the covenant under Moses in the thirteenth century B.C. The context of these words in worship is a renewal of the Old Covenant, very much as our eucharistic worship is a renewal of the New Covenant. In worship, the new generation becomes contemporaneous with the first generation. Such an event is not an ordinary occurrence. *It is a religious possibility*, an implication of liturgy, made possible by the Spirit, in worship.

Like the Old Covenant, the New is made "not with our fathers but with us, who are all of us alive' here this day." This continual renewal of the New Covenant, established by the liturgy and sacrifice of Christ our priest, is a possibility of worship in the Holy Spirit. When we worship, we "celebrate the memorial of our redemption. . . . Recalling his death, resurrection, and ascension, we offer you these gifts" (BCP, p. 363). Our time has been transformed into his time.

It is not simply that the moment of past revelation becomes present by the Spirit in worship. The time of future consummation also becomes present. Christian life is lived between the time when our Lord Jesus Christ "came to visit us in great humility" and "the last day, when he shall come again in glorious majesty to judge both the living and the dead" (BCP, p. 211). Christian worship occurs in a time which, regarded from an ordinary point of view, is between those times. But by the power of the Spirit, worship occurs in the presence of God, in a time when the Lord, crucified and risen, is present and when we share the coming victory of God, also known as present.

The presence of both past and future in the time of worship is expressed most clearly in Eucharistic Prayer D of the new Book of Common Prayer, although this transformation of time is implied at every Eucharist and indeed at every meeting of the Christian community to worship God:

> Father, we now celebrate this memorial of our redemption. Recalling Christ's death and his descent among the dead, *proclaiming* his resurrection and ascension to your right hand, *awaiting* his coming in glory; and offering to you, from the gifts you have given us, this bread and this cup, we praise you and we bless you. (BCP, p. 376; emphasis added)

Christ is known as our liturgy, sacrifice, priest, prayer, myth, and ritual, because he is present to us in worship, by the power of the Spirit through the transformation of time. It is God the Spirit who makes real the mystery of Christian worship.

Worship and Reconciliation

Liturgy not only implies the transformation of time, but the transformation of worshipers, and finally the transformation of the world. The liturgy, of course, does not do such things by itself. It is not magic. As God the Spirit works through the liturgy to become present and accessible to us, so God the Spirit works through the liturgy to lead us to reconciliation with our neighbors and with the world.

The ways by which God calls us to reconciliation are infinitely varied. Sometimes it is not through the liturgy at all. For some it has been initiated through a casual, even indifferent, attendance at church services. Whatever the means, the depth of Christian life is not achieved, even through the liturgy, unless it is internalized and takes root in a true change of heart.

On the other hand, this interior change, which moves us from preoccupation with ourselves to a life centered on God, must externalize itself in concrete ways. If I am not the center of the world, if all things are not for the enhancement of my life, if I am a child of God—and if all these things are similarly true of those who acknowledge the same God—then the texture and quality of relations between us who share this common Father is a matter of utmost importance. The life of those who truly worship together is community in Christ. Common worship, especially the Eucharist, is the sign of the unity which exists among us. More than this, it is the sign of judgment upon our sinful violations of unity; and even more than this, it is a source of nourishment as we press toward our common goal, which is Christ. We are fed by what we become. To borrow a phrase, "you are what you eat."

Worship in the Christian community, therefore, leads to acknowledgment of our guilt for breaking the community and to reconciliation with our brothers and sisters in Christ. Estranged neighbors always confront us with the need to set

aside our pride for their good, and for the good of the community as a whole. Penitence is one of the first implications
of the Christian liturgy. Penitence leads to reconciliation. Reconciliation with neighbors is a sign of our mutually being
drawn away from our self-centeredness into a centering on
Christ. Luther spoke of sin as a state of being "turned in on
one's self" (*incurvatus in se*). Christ enables us to escape the
tyranny of our egos and turn toward the world. Apart from
Christ, such a denial of the self is a type of madness. In him it
becomes the deepest fulfillment of the self, realized in communion (common union) with our neighbors. This insight
lies at the heart of the New Testament image of the Church as
the Body of Christ.

Where this sign of reconciliation is present, it is the distinctive sign of Christian discipleship and the hallmark of life in
Christ: "By this shall all men know that you are my disciples,
if you have love for one another" (Jn. 13:35). A true Christian
liturgy implies a reconciled community of faith. An individualistic approach to the sacraments can altogether avoid this
implication. In such an approach, the relation of individuals
to their neighbors has nothing to do with the liturgy. The
fundamental action takes place between the individual and
God. When this is the case, worship has no bearing on the
quality of life in the community. One worships wearing
spiritual blinders, so that one does not have to see the people
on either side. Yet if through the Christian liturgy, one is not
enabled to see Christ in one's neighbor, one has missed the
whole point. One of the most familiar passages of the New
Testament, the parable of the Last Judgment, indicates that
the very basis of God's judgment of us is our treatment of
others. "Lord, when did we see thee hungry and feed thee, or
thirsty and give thee drink? . . . And the King will answer
them, 'Truly, I say to you, as you did it to one of the least of
these my brethren you did it to me" (Mt. 25:37, 40).

The imperative of the liturgy is a commitment to reconciliation. Reception of the sacrament with such an intention is no
mere act of personal piety. It is the sign of our dependence on
him who is our unity and our peace. An indifferent reception
of the Eucharist, when we are not "in love and charity with

[our] neighbors" and don't even see the need to be, is a blatant refusal to discern the Lord's body (cf. 1 Cor. 11:29). Indifference to reconciliation as an implication of the liturgy is itself a judgment. It is no small thing to approach the altar of God.

Worship and Mission

As the liturgy leads to reconciliation with our neighbors already within the Christian community, it also leads to the evangelization of those not yet members of the Body of Christ. Mission is another consequence of worship. A popular name for the Eucharist among Roman Catholics and some Anglicans is *Mass*. The name establishes this connection. For it is taken from the short sentence which once stood at the end of the Latin liturgy, addressed by priest to people, *Ite, missa est.* "Go, it is the dismissal." *Mass* is the English form of the Latin *missa*. Mass is dismissal, sending into the world. Mass implies mission.

To speak in this way expresses a truth about Christian worship which we have encountered a number of times in these pages. Worship always has two phases: in one phase, the community gathers to celebrate its liturgy in the usual sense of the word, its praise and thanksgiving, its penitence and adoration in the presence of the crucified and risen Lord; in the other phase, the community lives in the world according to the love and power which come from him, in obedience and trust.

From our risen Lord, the church has received its apostolic commission: "Go therefore and make disciples of all nations, baptizing them in the name of the Father and of the Son and of the Holy Spirit, teaching them to observe all that I have commanded you; and lo, I am with you always, to the close of the age" (Mt. 28:19–20). The church exists to announce "to all nations" that the rule of God is at hand. This outreach of the Christian community to the whole world in the name of Jesus Christ has been characteristic of the church's life from the beginning. Without it, the church would not be the church. Liturgy which does not lead to evangelism is not authentic and does not communicate the power of the Spirit.

During the past hundred years or so the mission of the church has often been confused with the dissemination of Western culture and distorted by the dominance of American and European power. Under these circumstances the true quality of life in Christ made possible by Word and Sacrament has been communicated only with the greatest difficulty. Moreover Asian and African churches are themselves becoming missionary churches to an extraordinary degree. Consequently, the nature of missionary activity in our own church is going through a process of radical criticism and reformulation. We have learned that the mission of the church is directed at least as much to those who are near as to those who live in some distant place. It involves the self-giving love of Christian worshipers expressed in many more ways than in the gift of money alone. It involves a concern for men and women with various hungers and needs who live on our own street and in our own town. There can be no thought of giving up the missionary activity of the church, for the church in every time and place is essentially and irreducibly missionary. When we hear the word of Christ proclaimed in the liturgy and receive his life given for us, we accept a commission to give every person in every place accessible to us an opportunity to hear the same word and receive the same life. Authentic liturgy makes missionaries of us all.

Worship and Ministry

Such a deepened understanding of the implications of the liturgy makes us rethink many of our provisions for the external ordering of our common life. One of the most obvious areas where such rethinking is necessary is ministry.

For most people, the word *ministry* calls to mind ordained persons—bishops, priests, deacons. In fact, the word *ministry* has far broader reference than merely to the ordained. Its essential meaning originates in baptism. It pertains to every Christian person. Unfortunately in the course of the Christian centuries we have lost that association. The idea that every Christian is a minister comes to the ears of many as something strange and new.

We are heirs to a long tradition of clericalism, as we said in an earlier connection. We often picture the church as a group of active clerical suppliers to passive lay consumers, with the laity not as the basic category of church membership but as quite a secondary one. Actually the church *is* the laity—the *laos* ("people"). The church is the people of God. Within the *laos* there is an extraordinary diversity of ministries, each of which expresses some particular way in which a member of the body of Christ actualizes the Christian liturgy in the world.

Clergy, of course, have their distinctive roles to perform, and the focal role which clergy play in church services inevitably tends to emphasize the significance of clerical ministries. The prominence of the clerical office has developed to such a point, however, that the chief function of ordained persons, to *serve* the body, has become grossly obscured. At the worst periods of Christian history, the perversion has been complete. Laity have been seen as the servants of the clergy.

Today we are a long way from such an extreme. Yet clericalism lingers, for it appeals not only to clergy but to some lay persons as well. It is a tempting attitude for laity who want to be passive, either because they find security in having an omnicompetent oracle or because they do not want to accept the responsibilities of Christian life implied in their baptism. A living body requires the living participation of all its members. So too does the body of Christ.

Ministry is the activity of the entire body of Christ. Each person has a special ministry, shaped to fit the given reality of that person's life. Ministry is not the enactment of a predetermined pattern of action. An individual or a parish or a diocese may be called upon to minister in unexpected ways, since ministry is always a response to a unique situation. Ministry is the way in which individuals or communities respond to the persons or situations in which they find themselves, in obedience to the command proclaimed in the liturgy: to love others as Christ loved them. Ministry is not to another person at another time. It is here and now. It is not what we would do if we had greater resources or if the situation were somehow different. Ministry is what is done with existing resources in existing circumstances in obedience to Christ the Lord. If the person who crosses our path is hungry and our response is "I would feed you *if* I had more bread," then we have failed to minister in the name of Christ. These remarks about ministry may seem obvious, yet the clericalization of ministry has beclouded its essential character. When ministry is viewed primarily as the work of ordained persons, it comes to be understood almost exclusively as actions within the church, often as those ceremonial actions which ordained persons do. Thus the whole implication of liturgy for service to the world is lost.

It is of little value to aim criticism at the highly clericalized concept of the liturgy which dominated the Middle Ages and the Reformation. The Protestant preacher, as we have seen, was as highly clericalized a figure as the Roman priest. The problem was not with the liturgy in either case. The problem was more deep-rooted, a basic distortion in the idea of the church. The primitive community was genuinely an organic, priestly body, and its worship manifested this corporate character because its self-image was corporate.

This is not to question a legitimate role for ordained persons both in leading the liturgy and in enabling the priestly ministry of the whole people of God both to the church and to the world. When the particular ministries of clergy are seen in the context of the ministry of the whole church, as a service to the whole church for its life in the world, then the ordained priesthood emerges with its own integrity. It reminds the whole church, through Word and Sacrament, of the sources of its common life in Christ, so that all the members can be nourished and strengthened to fulfill their particular vocations and ministries.

These comments suggest that the active participation of the laity in the liturgy, which has been one of the principal tenets of the liturgical movement, is not merely whim or fad on the part of liturgists. It expresses the nature of the church as portrayed in the New Testament. St. Paul compared the church to a body made up of interdependent members. It is a society "from whom the whole body, joined and knit together by every joint with which it is supplied, when each part is working properly, makes bodily growth and upbuilds itself in love" (Eph. 4:16). This proper working of each part has to do primarily with the way each person does ministry in the world. But it has to do also with the way each person fulfills a liturgy in worship. When life is conceived in terms of the mutuality of all vocations within the church, and not in terms of the primacy of the clerical vocation, this mutuality within the common life must and will demand expression in the liturgical assembly. Liturgy leads to the ministry of the entire people of God in the world. Liturgy also expresses this mutual ministry.

It remains to be said that all ministry is related to Christ's own ministry of service. The very word *ministry* is derived from the Latin *minus,* lesser. The word calls to mind what Jesus said to his disciples:

> . . . whoever would be great among you must be your servant, and whoever would be first among you must be slave of all. For the Son of man came not to be served but to serve ["not to be ministered unto but to minister" as the King James Version runs], and to give his life as a ransom for many. (Mk. 10:43–45)

Like nearly everything else we have considered in our survey of Christian worship, ministry depends on Christ. He thought of his role as being that of a servant. Consequently, the church which he founded is a servant church. His body in the world, filled with his Spirit, moves from the service of God in the liturgy to the service of God in the world. The whole church was founded to minister, and to exercise its ministry in the spirit of Christ. Each member of the body has a special ministry which belongs to that person alone.

We have seen now how participation in liturgy has conse-quences for a person's life. It should lead to reconciliation with one's neighbors and the unity of the church. It should lead to involvement in mission, and so to reconciliation with the world. It should lead each Christian to regard life in the world as a ministry. Ministry is the means to reconciliation. It is also true that reconciliation, evangelism, and ministry deepen and intensify the liturgy. The reconciliation of church members to each other strengthens the bonds of love which bind Christians together. The corporate nature of the community, which we have already seen to play a decisive part as a ground of the liturgy, is enhanced. The mission of the church brings a larger and more varied chorus to join the praise of God. The implications of the expanded sense of ministry for the active participation of the laity in the liturgy are evident.

Thus, liturgy not only has consequences for life. Life has consequences for the liturgy. Christians move always from prayer and praise in the church to life and work in the world. The two activities, properly understood, flow into each other, and reinforce each other to the greater glory of God. When the connection is broken both worship and witness suffer.

Note

---

1. *The Hymnal 1940*, Hymn 80.

EPILOGUE
Living the Liturgy

We have now reached the end of our study. In retrospect, we can see that three themes have been woven into nearly all the previous chapters. These three themes may be said to constitute the warp of this book. The other material—the biblical and liturgical details, the theological interpretations— are its woof. Obviously both warp and woof are essential to any woven texture. But the warp is basic. These three themes constitute the underlying message of the foregoing pages. It may be helpful to mention them at the end, so that readers can see for themselves how much these ideas have influenced and shaped the whole of the study.

These three themes are: (1) the interdependence of liturgical worship and obedient life in the world—the people of God live their liturgy continuously; (2) the interdependence of corporate and individual worship—the individuality of Christian worshipers is heightened by their participation in the liturgy of the whole people; and (3) the richness and variety which is possible in Christian worship—the joyful unity of the people of God is not secured by uniformity of worship but by mutual love, trust, and faith; variety need not impair Christian unity.

The greatest shortcomings in Christian thought and charity often occur when well-intentioned Christians fail to acknowledge one of two mutually dependent sides of the truth. The themes we have identified might serve as illustrations of the point. They require that an even balance be kept between two emphases which at first glance might seem to be mutually exclusive.

1. Liturgy and Life

We have insisted, perhaps too frequently, that liturgy and life belong together. The title of the book, *Liturgy for Living*, holds them together. The New Testament, as we saw, uses the word *liturgy* exclusively to refer to the way Christians *live*. Only gradually was the word liturgy applied to church services and to the text of Christian *prayers*.

Once made, however, this identification of liturgy *only* with services of worship proved to be the stronger one. It has almost crowded out the older and original sense of the term—a life lived in the world, obedient to the sacrificial example of Jesus himself. When liturgy means a service of worship disconnected from the context in life which originally gave it its meaning, serious distortion occurs. In reaction against such a distortion of true worship, Christians have sometimes rejected liturgical worship altogether, in favor of purely worldly ethical obedience. The last decade, the tumultuous sixties, offered many examples of that rejection.

In this book we have sought to restore the mutual connection between liturgy and life. We have proposed the term *intensive liturgy* to describe what happens when Christians assemble to worship God, and the term *extensive liturgy* to describe what happens when Christians leave the assembly to conduct their daily affairs. The two are mutually dependent. By its intensive liturgies, the church encounters Christ as present in Word and Sacrament. Under these forms, Christians appropriate his example and the power which he makes available. To describe a liturgy in such terms, however, is to make its incompleteness obvious. One appropriates an example and its power only for a purpose. One leaves the intensive liturgy to live in accordance with the model and in the strength of the grace which it supplies.

As our intensive liturgies drive us into the world to do our extensive liturgies, so our extensive liturgies bring us back week by week to the Christian assembly, to seek God's presence once more under the embodied forms of Word and Sacrament. For the world is stronger than we are. By our own strength, we cannot long live up to Christ's example, nor can we get along without a renewal of spiritual power. Failures are frequent. Discouragement is always close. Need alone would return us to the unfailing source of renewal, given expression and made accessible by the liturgy of the church.

Not only need brings us back, to be sure; thanksgiving also brings us back. Our extensive liturgies are not only the story of failure, although failures are many; they are also the stories of success and triumph. To keep the record straight, and to make sure that we give God the credit due to God alone, we return to give him thanks.

To need and thanksgiving, among the motives which drive Christians to worship in their intensive liturgies, should be added adoration and joy. Finally, worship is an end in itself. Finally, liturgy is play. It is endless joy to add our voices to the praises on which God's people enthroned the Lord; and it is our final fulfillment to adore God for his beauty and majesty, to be "lost in wonder, love, and praise."

2. Corporate and Individual Worship

We have also insisted, perhaps too often, that liturgy is not merely a private affair between each individual and God. Neither is it a transaction between priest and God, which lay persons are privileged to watch, and from which they benefit, but in which they do not play an essential role. By way of contrast to both these views, caricatures (though recognizable ones) of Protestant and Catholic distortions of worship, we have insisted in this volume that worship is an affair of all the people of God, clergy and laity together, each in their own order.

In each section of our study, we have tried to show how this all-encompassing conception of worship has been given liturgical expression. We have also gone to some lengths to indicate that corporate worship does not mean the end of individual worship, but rather enhances it. Worship is not corporate *instead of* being individual. It is corporate *so that it can be* truly individual.

The Christian body is composed of separate selves. Yet individuals become who they are, not in isolation from their relationship with other individuals but because of those relationships. When we are redeemed by Christ, we cannot be extracted from our associations. We are redeemed in the context of our associations. God *saves* the world; he does not simply rescue individuals *from* the world.

Thus when we live our liturgies, either intensive or extensive, we do so as individual persons who are members of the body of Christ. Our participation in the congregation deepens our individuality. On the other hand, our individual lives, deepened and redeemed, forgiven and empowered by God, *together* compose the Church, the agent of God's will in the world. We worship both as individuals and as a corporate body. Both individual and corporate dimensions are essential to true Christian worship.

3. The Richness and Variety of Christian Worship

The third thread which has made up the warp of this book is the richness and variety of Christian worship. Anglicans have not believed for a long time, if we ever did, that unity is to be equated with uniformity. At least from the time of Queen Elizabeth I in the sixteenth century, the Church of England has been conceived as a "roomy" church. One major contribution of the Catholic revival of the nineteenth century was to introduce an even larger range of liturgical options, although sometimes at the cost of unity and harmony within our fellowship.

The new Book of Common Prayer attempts to strike a delicate balance between a core of common and irreplaceable texts on the one hand, and variety of expression and style on the other. It rests on the assumptions that the need of the emerging English nation in the sixteenth century for a stable and uniform state church has long since passed, that books are easily obtainable, and that literacy is common. The church can therefore afford to encourage far more variation than it could at the beginning.

Yet Anglican experience has taught us also the value of fixed prayers and a uniform translation of the psalms which can sink deep into our hearts, leaving an invaluable store of strength, beauty, and wisdom. Some invariable liturgical forms and unchanging words are of incalculable value in the formation of Christian lives. The church must preserve the liturgical heritage in which generations of Anglicans have found their identity.

In the resulting balance in the new Prayer Book between the fixed and the optional, between the changing and the invariable, between freedom and order, the American Episcopal Church hopes that all its people in a number of different styles will be able to worship God with the freedom of the primitive Christians, with the splendor of the medieval church, with the sober dignity of the Reformation, and with a simplicity and grace all its own.

The Lord is in his holy temple. Come, let us adore him.

· 6 ·

The Christian Moral Vision

- Should you "be good to yourself" or is that concept bad for a Christian to deal with?
- Do you really believe that your body is, as Scripture tells us, "the temple of the Holy Spirit"?
- If you follow a religion that does not preach abstention from alcohol as a tenet of church membership, is it all right for you to get drunk once in a while?
- If you follow a path of conduct that does harm to no one—except perhaps yourself—are you being a "good Christian"?

The Christian Moral Vision does not pull any punches. It is a frank, open, and hard look at life as it is lived now. The author does not avert his eyes from situations that might be considered outside the realm of the church by some. For *The Christian Moral Vision* has a point of view that would suggest looking everywhere and asking a great many questions. It tells the religious and specifically Biblical grounding of Christian ethical and moral views, it deals with the moral issues that come up in the course of everyone's day-to-day life, and it spots the larger ethical and moral issues of—or arising from—our institutions. This is a very "unchurchy" book and, at the same time, a very religious book.

The selection included here from *The Christian Moral Vision* is as straightforward and basic as anything could be. It is from the section of the book called "Moral Issues in Personal Living" and it is called "Running Your Own Life." And that is exactly what it is about. It is a provocative piece because it leaves no place to hide. The author believes in the totality of the Christian commitment and the wholeness of life. And so he is telling us that there is no issue in our lives—no issue at all—that we can claim has nothing to do with Christianity. If we are Christians and it has to do with us, it has to do with Christianity.

Most of the things we have read about in the newspaper and in magazines are here. Familiar, almost nightmarish phrases float through the text—"Me-ism," "Instant Gratification," alcoholism, drug abuse, gambling—they are all here. But this is not a depressing catalogue of pious glosses on human vice. The implication is that the worst vice of all may well be to deceive ourselves about what we are really doing with our lives and our bodies. And somehow it is all the more frightening when the scent of fire and brimstone and the devils with pointed horns and pitchforks are taken away, and we are made to look at things as they are without the melodrama of leering villains and beset heroes and abused maidens.

The Christian Moral Vision, as you will gather from this selection, asks the reader to be honest with himself or herself. It seems the best way to begin an enterprise as important as that of being a Christian.

Running Your Own Life

"Love your neighbor as yourself." That is the norm for Christian living. It implies that love of self is natural and legitimate. But how am I to go about loving myself? Are there ethical issues in the running of my own life? Or is what I do by myself, to myself, strictly my own business as long as I do not step on anyone else's toes?

This question takes on a special significance in our individualistic age. In our society, people are burdened with a heightened sense of self that, while legitimate at its best, tends to limit our vision and cut us off from the world outside the self.

The Temple of the Holy Spirit

The Bible knows no such individualistic perspective, for it sees human life lived out under the searching gaze of the Almighty. No human act is without significance. Everything we are or do, think or feel, is subject to divine judgment. Paul expresses the biblical view most succinctly:

> Do you not know that your body is a temple of the Holy Spirit within you, which you have from God? You are not your own; you were bought with a price. So glorify God in your body (1 Cor. 6:19–20).

Our lives are a gift which we receive in trust. We are accountable to God for our stewardship of that gift, just as in

95

the biblical parable the servants who received talents from their master were held responsible for their use of those talents (Mt. 25:14–30).

Decisions about what we will do with our lives are inevitably shaped by our religious convictions. If you believe that you owe your life to God and are responsible to him for the use you make of it, you will make one kind of choice. You will make quite different choices if you see your life as a mere biological accident, without meaning or purpose.

ME-ISM

Journalist Tom Wolfe has called this the "Me Decade."[1] He was referring, of course, to the widespread preoccupation with the self that seems characteristic of our society. It is typified by such popular book titles as *How to Be Your Own Best Friend, Winning through Intimidation,* and *Looking out for Number One.* The proliferation of modish self-help therapies is another indication of what Wolfe is describing.

Self-preoccupation in itself is nothing new. We humans have always shown a tendency to look out for ourselves. But throughout the Christian era we have been taught that selfishness and self-centeredness are manifestations of human sinfulness. In the past our religious convictions have led us to be ashamed of our selfishness and to confess it as sin.

Today, however, we are witnessing a militant repudiation of altruism and concern for others. Our society has made a virtue of this self-preoccupation.

To be sure, the Gospel does not condemn self-love. The commandment, after all, is to love your neighbor as yourself, not instead of yourself. Paul is even more explicit about self-affirmation when he points out, "No man ever hates his own flesh, but nourishes and cherishes it" (Eph. 5:29). This fact deserves to be emphasized, because some Christian teaching has tended to downgrade the self. Love of neighbor has sometimes been interpreted to mean that it is sinful to look after our own interests. Humility has often been understood to mean that we should regard ourselves as no-account worms.

The Christian understanding of the self begins with the affirmation of the self. We are right to assert our own dignity and worth. We are made in God's image; Christ died for us. God loves us. We are important; we count.

If you really believe that, then you have no need to be constantly taking your psychological pulse, wondering, "How am I doing?" "What do they really think of me?" If you can honestly and genuinely affirm yourself, then you can stop worrying about yourself and get on to more important things. This is what lies behind Jesus' promise that only by losing your life will you find it (Mt. 10:39).

INSTANT GRATIFICATION

Our individualistic culture puts a high premium on the gratification of every desire. We want what we want when we want it; usually we want it right now. The world of commerce constantly reminds us that we have an unqualified right to satisfy our every appetite. The world of instant mass communication turns its heavy guns on us to stimulate those appetites, so that we are almost required to want more and more all the time.

Television commercials, newspaper and magazine advertisements, easy credit, and a bewildering array of products designed to make us look good, feel good, smell good; products designed to give us good flavors and good sounds, ease and comfort—all of these conspire to convince us that the good life is a matter of making the right purchases. At the same time they undercut our capacity for sustained effort, self-discipline, and self-sacrifice.

One striking product of the cult of instant gratification is the "fan." The fan is passive. The fan craves entertainment not participation—or rather, participation by proxy. Under the impact of fandom, sports have become show biz, with winning the only suitable climax. You don't have to play the game or even know anything about it. You identify with your team by buying an imitation team jersey with your hero's number on it. At the championship games it is the fans who shout, "We're number one! "

Pop music fans buy records, pay hefty prices to attend

overcrowded concerts, collect posters of the superstars and imitate not their musical achievements but their hair and dress styles. Fans play records, not instruments, because to play an instrument with any skill you have to practice, and everybody knows practice is "no fun."

Because we demand instant gratification, we no longer save up to buy things the way our parents did. We buy first and pay later so that we do not have to wait or set priorities for ourselves. Thanks to instant credit, we can have everything instantly. Most Americans would consider it unthinkable to do without something they want merely because they cannot afford it.

The moral issue raised by the cult of instant gratification is a difficult one to state. There is nothing inherently evil in sports, pop music, or entertainment itself. The evil arises when we become dependent on these things, when we cannot do without them, when we allow our lives to be shaped by forces outside ourselves. When we can get whatever we want whenever we want it, when we can avoid all pain and struggle, then without ever realizing it, we begin to lose control of our own lives. We lose the capacity for sustained personal effort; we lose the capacity to endure deprivation; we lose the ability to postpone present pleasure for the sake of future good.

When that happens, we miss out on some of life's more significant experiences. Even the goods and pleasures get stale in a hurry, leaving us restless and dissatisfied. Instant gratification leaves us without the personal resources to struggle and grow.

Paul was saying something like this when he described his own life in terms of an athlete in training:

> Every athlete exercises self-control in all things. They do it to receive a perishable wreath, but we an imperishable. Well, I do not run aimlessly, I do not box as one beating the air, but I pommel my body and subdue it, lest after preaching to others I myself should be disqualified (1 Cor. 9:25–27).

This perspective undergirds the ascetical tradition in Christianity. In some ages, that tradition has been dominant;

in others, it has been neglected. Most Americans regard asceticism with faint embarrassment. It smells like Puritanism, the neurotic denial of the world and the good things in it.

A reaffirmation of Christian asceticism does not mean, however, that we have to opt for the excesses 'of the Puritan temperament. It does not mean that Christians should renounce the genuinely good things of life. Anglicans have always stood within the world-affirming tradition of Christianity; that commitment needs to be maintained.

The strength of the ascetical tradition is its implicit protest against selfishness, acquisitiveness, and competitive striving. It calls us to self-discipline that will enable us to take responsible control of our own lives. It can free us from the pressures of a culture that has brought consumption to the brink of self-destructiveness.

We can cultivate a certain skepticism about the claims and promises dished out by the hucksters of the mass media. We can learn to sit loose to the trivial goods and pleasures that we are constantly told we cannot do without. We can achieve a balance in our lives, yielding neither to the hard sell of the pleasure peddlers nor the contrary temptation of joyless world-renunciation. We can take responsibility for the way we use our time, our energy, our money, testing every choice by our commitment to live an authentic and responsible life before the God who is the source of that life.

FAITH AND HEALTH

Your body can tell a great deal about you. When you "sit up and take notice," your body is saying that you are actively involved in what is going on. When you yawn and fidget, squirm and doze, your body is saying that you are bored to death. Conversely, your treatment of your body says something about your deepest convictions. The slogan of the high-liver—"Live fast, die young, and leave a good-looking corpse"—captures the profound cynicism of those for whom life has no meaning or significance.

By contrast, Christians believe that taking care of our bodies is a religious obligation. How are we supposed to do that? Obviously, we should not abuse our bodies, but we should not coddle ourselves either. We humans, apparently, function best when we do not have it too good. We need nourishing food, of course, but overnourishment is hazardous to our health. Simple foods, we are beginning to learn, are best for the body.

Most religions have advocated fasting as a spiritual discipline. In our society, people diet rather than fast, and they do it for cosmetic rather than spiritual purposes. Dieting can be joyless and monotonous, but fasting is a different matter. We fast only at specific times and seasons; at other times, we are called to feast instead. We ought to be able to do both with equal enthusiasm, as gourmet-theologian Robert Capon has suggested: "When you fast, FAST; and when you eat, EAT." The rhythm of both activities can save us from gluttony and from compulsive calorie counting.

In passing, let it be noted that there is no inherent superiority in either weight or food intake. Thin is not necessarily more commendable than fat. Obesity can be a moral issue when it springs from compulsive eating, or from simple greed. Otherwise, people should be able to affirm their own body types without suffering condemnation by other people with smaller waistlines.

Our freedom from physical labor presents us with similar spiritual hazards. One of the greatest achievements of our technological society is the extent to which it has freed us from brute labor. The increased power available to each of us, even with the increased cost of energy, makes it possible for us to expend less and less physical energy every year.

But this sedentary form of life has its own hazards. We are discovering that the relaxed comfort of our physical surroundings is unhealthy. Most of us do not get enough exercise and our bodies literally waste away as the years go by. The body can cope with fatigue fairly well; it copes less well with stress, to which we are ever more frequently subjected.

Fortunately many people in recent years have come to realize the extent of their deprivation. As a result, the nation has gone on an exercise binge. Exercise has become fashionable. Walking, running, tennis, health clubs, calisthenics, TV exercise programs all serve to affirm the value of physical exercise. We will no doubt reap even more benefits when we learn to build physical activity into our daily lives: using our automobiles less, walking more, throwing away some of our more exotic labor-saving appliances.

Our rediscovery of the value of exercise is a positive good. But like all good things, it breeds its own contradictions and distortions. The cultivation of one's own body can become idolatrous. One physical fitness fanatic was quoted recently as saying, "You have to take care of your body. It's all you have." Thus an activity that, for the Christian, can be a conscientious form of stewardship can also be distorted into a form of self-preoccupation, just as a legitimate concern for good health can become the obsession known as hypochondria.

Once again, then, we are driven back to the recognition of the importance of what we believe and the reasons for what we do. Many of these activities are morally neutral. The meaning of the act depends upon the convictions that underlie it, the motives that inspire it, the intentions that shape it.

For the Christian, the body is a temple of the Holy Spirit. Therefore we will take good care of it. We will seek to keep it under control, because it is God's gift to us and we would use our bodies in the ways that God intends. We were bought for a price and we would not want that sacrifice to be wasted.

The Conventional Vices

At an earlier time, the discussion of Christian behavior would have focused on certain vices: drinking, smoking, gambling. In some circles even dancing, card playing, and movies would have been condemned as "worldly amusements." We have largely rejected such prohibitions because we have regarded them as petty and meaningless. That rejection may have been premature; perhaps the time has come for us to reassess our attitude toward some of these matters, not in the spirit of the killjoy but in frank recognition of the consequences of our behavior for ourselves and for others as well.

ALCOHOL: PROHIBITION AND TEMPERANCE

The crusade against the use of alcoholic beverages is one of the most persistent features of the American religious scene. It is an oft-told story. Church members launched a temperance movement which later changed its emphasis from temperance to total abstinence. Though working first by persuasion, the movement soon changed its tactic to working for laws to forbid the use of alcoholic beverages. The movement reached its zenith with the adoption of the Eighteenth Amendment to the Constitution in 1919, which ushered in the era of national prohibition, the "noble experiment."

Some reform was surely in order, but Prohibition was strong medicine. Americans were the hardest drinkers on the face of the earth. Foreign visitors frequently reported, with awe and amazement, that an American would reach for his whiskey jug the first thing on rising in the morning, even before breakfast. It is no accident that our first major internal conflict was the Whiskey Rebellion, a protest against a measure to tax whiskey.

The effects of prohibition were ambiguous. We have all heard that prohibition touched off a decade of bathtub gin, bootlegging, speakeasies, gangsters—the Roaring Twenties, in brief. The conventional wisdom maintains that, since alcohol was "forbidden fruit," many people, especially the young, began drinking when otherwise they would not have.

That may (or may not) be true, but it is also true that, even long after the repeal of prohibition in 1933, we had not returned to the high level of alcoholic consumption that had been reached before prohibition. Also, when alcohol came back, it did so under many severe restrictions, most of which had not previously existed.

Alcohol made its biggest comeback after World War II as our postwar affluence increased the amount and kind of drinking. Scotch and bourbon replaced the cheaper blended whiskies. The martini reigned supreme. Business, government, and university ran on alcohol. Lush lunches, cocktail parties, receptions, meetings—all were well oiled, but not by oil.

Restrictions on the use of alcohol began to break down. Liquor by the drink became universally available; Sunday drinking spread. Churches that opposed drinking were no longer attacked; they were merely dismissed as "uncool." Drinking became pervasive in American society.

The results of this development were predictable. Alcoholism is now a major health problem. Alcohol is involved in fully half of our fatal automobile accidents. Excessive drinking often results in poor work performance; it sometimes leads to mental illness.

The Episcopal Church was never prominently involved in the prohibition movement. Most Episcopalians have accepted wine as a gift of God, to be used with thanksgiving. The wine of the Eucharist serves as a symbol of God's blessing on the fruit of the vine.

As a result, it has been easy to identify the Episcopal Church as "the drinking man's church" and the Gospel as liberation from petty rules such as "Don't drink." Friend and foe alike have tirelessly repeated witticisms about "whiskey-palians" and stale jokes like, "Wherever there are four Episcopalians, there is sure to be a fifth." Episcopalians have taken a perverse pride in such remarks, which seemed to testify to the sophistication of the church and its freedom from petty moralism.

But less often mentioned is the price of it all. Alcohol produces a major portion of the pastoral problems of most parish clergy. Alcoholism among the clergy is itself a major issue. The use of alcohol has increased in the life of the church itself. Parish meetings, diocesan events, conferences, and other occasions almost always include a "happy hour," when drinks are served. It has come to be *de rigueur* to include alcohol in any ecclesiastical social function.

It seems clear that, as a people, Americans drink too much. We create a climate in which others are encouraged to drink and to increase their drinking. Our overuse of alcohol brings unnecessary grief to ourselves and others. Perhaps we can defend that use but, in the light of its consequences, the burden of proof must rest upon the user.

At the very least, we can scale down our consumption of

alcohol if it seems to be getting to be a problem. We can substitute wines for liquor. We can offer attractive nonalcoholic alternatives when we entertain. We can abstain from alcohol for particular periods. We could even risk our reputation for sophistication by entertaining without alcohol. If you have a problem in your own use of alcohol, your most responsible decision would be to face the fact and, if necessary, to get professional help to deal with it.

As a nation, we seem to be getting over our post prohibition drinking binge. In some sophisticated circles, it has become stylish to cut down on drinking. The Episcopal Church may be able to exercise some leadership in this direction. Since it has never been identified with prohibition or total abstinence, and since it has done much to make drinking respectable in religious circles, the Episcopal Church can perhaps do as much to make nondrinking respectable once more. One need not make a case for teetotalism, but there is a case to be made for temperance and restraint in the use of something that turns out to be both a gift from God and a hazard to health.

DRUG ABUSE

Narcotic substances of one sort or another have been on the scene for a long time, but for the most part their use has been confined to relatively small and isolated groups in the society: the urban poor, immigrants, jazz musicians, the occasional physician who gets hooked on morphine. For the past twenty years, however, we have seen a militant drive to encourage the use of drugs as a way of expanding the mind, of encountering a higher level of reality.

The moral issues involved in the use of such substances are similar to those involved in the use of alcohol. In both cases, use of the substance can create dependency, robbing the self of its freedom. Both can be destructive of physical and mental health. In both cases, one's individual behavior can have tragic consequences for others in one's life: family, friends, coworkers.

Society, however, treats drugs differently from the way it

treats alcohol. We have given up the attempt to prohibit the use of alcohol, but still prohibit the use of marijuana, along with such drugs as morphine, cocaine, and heroin as well as the more esoteric chemicals like LSD and PCP. There has been, for some years, a spirited debate over whether marijuana use should be made legal.

Four arguments are adduced in favor of legalizing marijuana. Tests indicate that marijuana may be no more dangerous than alcohol. If marijuana were legal, users would be shielded from contact with pushers of more dangerous drugs which would still be illegal. The government could control the quality of legal marijuana, protecting users from contamination by toxic substances. Finally, if marijuana were legalized, the government would reap huge benefits from taxes, which are now evaded by illegal operators.

These arguments are persuasive, if not entirely convincing. Those who oppose legalization argue that it would encourage greater use of marijuana, especially by the young. Not everyone agrees that marijuana has been proven safe; the experimental data is sparse and rather inconclusive. Finally, if marijuana were legal, it would probably be marketed by the same kind of sophisticated advertising techniques that have made us a nation of tobacco smokers.

Young people claim, with some justification, that in the past, so-called experts exaggerated the danger of marijuana. As a result, they are inclined to disregard any warnings about the dangers of any drug. Nevertheless the issue is sensitive, precisely because so many young people are lured into the use of dangerous drugs whose dangers they do not understand.

Recent research indicates that marijuana may be more dangerous in the long run than its users realize. It is undeniably hazardous for adolescents who are in an especially vulnerable state of personal development. Marijuana encourages passivity, makes it hard for young persons to concentrate, and inhibits their ability to cope with stressful mental activity or interpersonal relationships. If criminal sanctions are removed from marijuana use, some means will have to be found to discourage its use by the young.

Beyond the matter of dangerous drug abuse is a deeper moral issue in our whole society's casual use of chemicals in order to provide a short cut to health, beauty, and a good night's sleep. When advertising exalts the use of legal drugs to provide for our minds and bodies, it is easy to see how young people can be seduced by the claims of "mind expanding" drugs. It is even easier to see why young people in poor urban neighborhoods turn to hard drugs as a way of escaping an unbearable environment, however briefly and at whatever cost.

Obviously the Christian moral presumption is against the use of potentially harmful drugs. Of course we would recommend extreme caution in approaching them. But what can be done about drug abuse? Since it is irrational behavior to begin with, it is difficult to see how a user is going to be reasoned out of the habit. Caution, likewise, is a difficult attitude to convey to young people who are convinced that they are indestructible.

In many communities, church groups have sponsored drug abuse programs that seek to help people over their dependency on dangerous drugs. Such projects can convey to the drug user the loving concern of the Christian community and can offer resources to enable them to cope with their own problems. Beyond that, when someone close to us develops a drug dependency, rather than sitting in judgment upon them, we can surround them with care and support. If we ourselves should fall victim to drug dependency, we can seek for personal support and professional help in the Christian community.

THE SMOKING CONTROVERSY

While tobacco smoking is not nearly so serious an issue as drugs or alcohol, it confronts us with similar moral questions. Down through the years many traditional Protestant groups have frowned on smoking, but there has never been a major crusade to make it illegal. Since the sale of cigarettes is forbidden to minors, young people regard smoking as something like a rite of passage, a sign that one is now big enough to participate in real, grown-up vices.

Advertising has been largely responsible for making tobacco smoking a major phenomenon in American culture. Smoking has been pictured as an indispensable adjunct to the stylish life, or as part of the total life of the outdoor "he man." We have already seen how the ads that featured the attractive, sophisticated woman with a cigarette have made smoking acceptable behavior for women. "You've come a long way, Baby," the ad chortles. So have the tobacco companies, as today nearly as many women as men have become regular smokers.

But antismoking forces have received massive aid and comfort from an unexpected source. The United States Surgeon General has reluctantly reported that cigarette smoking is statistically associated with a high incidence of lung cancer. Later reports indicate that it contributes to heart and other lung diseases as well. As a result, cigarette commercials have been banned from the air waves, while cigarette ads and packaging are required to carry a warning that smoking may be harmful to your health.

Nonsmoking is now back in style and nonsmokers have risen up to put smokers on the defensive. Air lines are now required to provide nonsmoking areas on every flight. Smoking is prohibited in many public buildings. Restaurants sometimes offer nonsmoking areas.

Now that it has become fashionable to give up smoking, a whole new industry has grown up, claiming the ability, for a fee, to help people kick the habit. It is the difficulty of stopping that highlights the moral dimension of the smoking habit.

With the health hazards involved in smoking reasonably well known and well documented, the Christian moral presumption would be against smoking. Still, the decision must be made by the individual involved. There is no justification for moralistic pressure being brought to bear on smokers by nonsmokers, especially the militant ex-smoker. It is reasonable to let smokers know when their smoking causes discomfort or distress. Beyond that measure of self-protection, nonsmokers have no right to second guess the moral choice made by the person who, having considered the risks, still elects to continue smoking for the sake of the pleasure it provides.

GAMBLING

Gambling has a long history in this country, going back to horse racing, cock fighting, turkey shoots, and public lotteries in the Colonial period. For most of our national history, however, it has been forbidden by law, except under stringently controlled conditions.

For a long time Nevada was the only state to permit casino gambling. The incredible success of the gaming tables of Las Vegas has led to the introduction of gambling to older resorts such as Atlantic City. Gambling has become respectable. Even more, it has become a flourishing business, showing up as a growth stock on the New York Stock Exchange.

The general attitude of the public seems to be, "People are always going to gamble, so why not make it legal and tax it, using the money for legitimate public purposes?" In that spirit, a number of states now operate public lotteries, while New York operates its own system of off-track betting.

Churches opposed these new laws when they were first proposed, but in most instances they have lost the battle to prevent the introduction of legalized gambling. Today gambling is so widely accepted that newspapers regularly carry the current betting odds on weekly football games. Despite religious scruples, gambling, it would seem, has become a part of the American way of life.

And why not? Why not remove the legal restrictions from practices that many people find unobjectionable? When gambling is legal, only those who approve of it need to participate in it. Those opposed can simply decline to gamble. Even if the state itself runs a lottery, what is wrong with that if the money is used for good causes?

Well, a funny thing happened on the way to the lottery.

During the debates on state lotteries, ambitious claims were often made concerning the amount of money to be made for the state. The lottery would support the schools, pay the deficit, and still make it possible to lower taxes because there were, presumably, millions upon millions of people out there just waiting to gamble their money away.

Things have not turned out exactly that way. The income from most state lotteries is far below expectations and I am willing to bet that it will continue to be. Gambling fever does not seem to run as high as we once thought, at least not as far as state lotteries are concerned.

The next step could have been predicted. The state-operated gambling enterprises now engage in heavy advertising to promote their wares. Maryland sponsors TV spots that proclaim, "You have to play to win!" New York advertises Off-Track Betting in billboards and subway ads that cry out, "Get a horse! "

While we may concede that it is legitimate for the state to take advantage of our human weaknesses, it is quite different when the state uses its prestige and its resources to act as a pusher, to lead people into gambling who might not otherwise have been tempted.

In what way does gambling violate the Christian demand to love, or even the Christian obligation to take reasonable care of oneself? After all, it is merely a form of amusement. You could spend a day at the races, pay your admission, buy refreshments, bet on every race, and lose all your money without spending much more than you might at some other form of amusement. If you can afford to spend the money and you enjoy the day, what is wrong?

Nothing is wrong with that. But that situation does not describe the way most gamblers gamble. There is a compulsive element in gambling that makes it dangerous because it so easily gets out of hand. Anyone associated with a serious gambler will tell you that the lure of easy winning quickly overcomes all reason, all argument, all caution. Many a family has fallen into financial ruin because a parent has become hooked on gambling. Gambling constitutes what traditional moral theology called "an occasion of sin." It can be dangerously habit forming and the victim seldom realized its power until it is too late.

For most people, gambling never reaches this stage. Participating in the office football pool is certainly an innocuous form of amusement. A weekly fifty-cent lottery ticket is hardly the road to perdition. But it is important to know what we are doing and what the costs may be. American society is developing toward gambling a rather casual and sentimental attitude which needs to be reexamined if we are to be serious in our commitment to live according to the law of love and the responsible use of ourselves and our resources.

The Corporate Dimensions of Individual Choices

The issues we have been discussing are intensely personal because they affect how we choose to live our own lives, use our own bodies, make our own choices. They have their social dimension, however, for we do not live to ourselves alone. We have seen how society shapes our moral choices, whether in a general sort of way by creating a certain moral climate, or in more specific ways like the promotional advertising that leads us to spend our time and money in a particular fashion.

At the same time, our personal choices have social consequences. My decision to gamble, for example, helps to create a social climate favorable to gambling and may lead others to take it up. If I serve drinks in my home, I lend respectability to drinking and may lead others to indulge.

Moreover, if I become addicted to any of these substances or activities, I will affect the lives of those about me. If my health suffers or my personality deteriorates, my family, my friends, and my coworkers will have to pay some of the price. In making decisions about my personal life, I cannot leave these people out of consideration.

At the same time, those people constitute a source of health, strength, and healing power. If I should become overwhelmed by addiction to one of the conventional vices, if

I lose the capacity to help myself, I am not therefore alone. I can reach out for help and support to those who care about me.

All of us, at one time or another, need help in coping with the cares and burdens of our personal lives. Christian humility is that virtue which enables us to see ourselves as we really are, with all our limitations and shortcomings. It can enable us to ask for help and support when we need it. Pride closes us off from the possibility of help from other people; humility opens us up to it. In the fellowship of the Christian community, we get by with a little help from our friends. Love dictates that we give them the chance to be helpful.

Note

1. Tom Wolfe, "The Me Decade and the Third Great Awakening," *Mauve Gloves and Madmen, Clutter & Vine* (New York: Bantam Books, 1977), pp. 111–147.

· 7 ·

Living in the Spirit

- What are we really expressing when we say at the end of a prayer, "Through Jesus Christ Our Lord"?
- Do you consider yourself to be a "spiritual" person? If you do, why? If you don't, why not?
- How often do you pray? Where do you pray? Why do you pray?

Living in the Spirit, the final volume in The Church's Teaching Series, is the one that may well contain the most surprises for contemporary people, even for those who consider themselves religious. Spirituality, the delicate, intricate involvement of the human soul with God, has until fairly recent years been considered to be a relationship that existed only for monks and nuns and the rare layperson with special gifts. Regular churchgoers, one was tempted to believe, had little to do with the life of the Spirit. And then in the latter part of the 1960s and in the 1970s, young people became attracted to spiritual pursuits, some of the pursuits good, many of them trivial, a few of them downright bad. But the word spirituality was back among us after many years of confinement in seminaries and other theoretically pious institutions. For better or worse—probably better—Christians were being asked to say, in effect, if they were spiritual beings. The authors of *Living in the Spirit* would probably be inclined to say, if asked, that an aware Christian has no choice about "being spiritual" or "not being spiritual." We have a relationship with the Holy Spirit that we are born to, and we have no choice in the matter. If we obstinately refuse to deal with it, we may be cheating ourselves and our lives of much richness—but that is beside the point, or perhaps it's not.

The selection from *Living in the Spirit* which follows is called "Praying in the Spirit." It opens with a phrase you may want to remember: "We are made after the image of God, and because of this our spirit responds spontaneously to his Spirit. Prayer is precisely the response of spirit to Spirit." The selection goes on to examine the essential meaning of prayer from every angle, making it as understandable as a human heartbeat.

Although this selection and all of *Living in the Spirit* is about a mystery there is nothing mysterious about the approach, for the point of view of the authors is that the spiritual life of a human being is as inevitable and natural as his or her physical life and rhythms. The barriers to understanding have more to do with language than they do with proclivities and dispositions. Few of us *think* of ourselves as being SPIRITUAL. But few people would deny that there are moments and experiences in their lives that transcend, that go beyond the usual. Call it what you like but its meaning is to be found in terms of the Holy Spirit.

Praying in the Spirit

We are made after the image of God, and because of this our spirit responds spontaneously to his Spirit. Prayer is precisely this response of spirit to Spirit. We are, as it were, most at home when we are in tune with the Spirit of Christ.

Nothing was ever quite the same after Christ. What he revealed was something about us. Through him we see that we are deep and inexhaustible mysteries related to and destined for God himself. God's deference and wonderful love are shown to us in Christ. The final tag we place at the end of our prayers, "Through Jesus Christ Our Lord," is, therefore, of vital importance. It is the key to a proper understanding of what makes Christian prayer Christian. We are claiming that all our being and doing is in and through him.

As we have seen, prayer is not, at its heart, one activity among many. When we talk about prayer in its broadest sense, we are using a word to describe a person's whole orientation or *style*. We might say that prayer is an expression of the whole person. Christian prayer, of course, is much more than a matter of style, much more than mere personal expression.

The impulse (in all people) to pray is an expression of the human heart towards some kind of end or fulfillment. It is a stretching out towards something or someone beyond us that promises us integrity and a sense of purpose, or that at least holds out to us the promise of an integrity we feel we have lost. The Christian understands that the human being is basically drawn towards God. All our desiring, all our longing, however misguided or corrupt, points to this one end. This end is called in the Christian tradition the *summum bonum* (the greatest good), the *visio dei* (the vision of God). It is beyond words. It is like being in love for the first time. The *summum bonum* and the *visio dei* point to a love affair with God that defies description. This love affair is *through Jesus Christ, Our Lord.*

When we throw ourselves enthusiastically into a relationship of faith and love with Christ, we find our true identity. Then our prayer becomes a movement of love towards God and the expression of our whole person. This is "to know that we are who we are, because *another* is who he is." This *Other* in our midst to whom we are intimately related is Christ. We have now identified this *otherness within* with which we began, as the presence of God himself; Father, Son, and Holy Spirit. It is this *Other* that binds us all together. When we are "in Christ," we are also intimately linked to one another. We are also copartners with everything God has made. This is what it means to be human.

A serious criticism leveled at those of us involved in a Christian life of prayer is that we tend to be very passive with regard to the social and political problems facing the human race. In classical terms this was called *a contempt for the world.* Yet Christian spirituality, which is truly rooted in Christ, has a passion and concern for wholeness, and this continually reaches out to the world in all its misery and pain.

The reason is simple. The Christian sees every human being, and indeed the whole human race, as the Temple of the Holy Spirit. Every individual is, potentially at least, the dwelling place of God. When we begin to see that fact and try to act on it, we realize the fantastic social and political dimensions of living in the Spirit.

There is, however, validity to the criticism that many Christians have made prayer the excuse for withdrawal from, and noninvolvement with, the world. To do this is to misunderstand who Christ really is.

All these criticisms, however, collapse in the light of the lives of those whom the church regards as great Christians. The saints are not, for the most part, antisocial, nor do they deny the ordinary course of human events as the supreme vehicle of meaning. The encounter with Christ always makes us reach out to the world and to one another.

Where are we to turn for guidance? What does the Christian tradition have to offer us with regard to our growth in the Spirit?

Prayer Is a Gift and a Movement towards Wholeness in Christ: It Is an Event of the Holy Spirit

Prayer is something given, and it is given by God, the Holy Spirit. This cannot be said often enough. It is like the air we breathe. It is necessary and unavoidable—simply there for our use. Prayer has something to do with breath, with breathing, with that which keeps us alive. It is something we don't think about most of the time. Many children are, at some point, terrified on going to bed at night, lest they forget to breathe while half-asleep or asleep. Children don't "forget," but the thought of not breathing is disturbing. So to compare prayer with the air we breathe throws light on its meaning. Spirit responds to spirit. God breathes his breath into us. That is what the Spirit is: breath that brings the body to life.

> . . . you take away their breath [spirit],
>   and they die and return to their dust.
>
> You send forth your Spirit, and they are created;
>   (Ps. 104:30–31)[1]

A Buddhist teacher once showed his pupil the importance of the desire for love and knowledge. He took the young man down to the river and pushed his head under the water and held it there until the pupil struggled to the surface

frightened and gasping for air. "Until you long for enlightenment in the same way that you struggled for air, it will never
be given you." Our longing for the Holy Spirit in prayer is
not unlike our struggling for air in order to live.

The spirit or breath is freely given, and the giver is God.
He gives and he takes away. It is not in our power. The Spirit
is not something we possess, though we may resist its power
or use it for evil purposes. All power, including spiritual
power, is from God, and we can misuse it. Jesus himself was
tempted to do this in the desert.

So the Spirit is given to us. He constitutes our very being.
We are most ourselves when our spirit is open to the Holy
Spirit, when the breath of God becomes our breath. Alas, we
are not always true to ourselves. To say that all life is spiritual
is like saying that all life (to *be* life) is alive. Christ makes us
who we *are*. To say that all life is spiritual is to say that all life
(to *be* life) is in Christ.

Prayer: the Movement towards Wholeness, Healing, and Holiness

So ours is a movement towards wholeness in Christ, and it
should not surprise us that the words *wholeness* and *healing*
come from the same root. Our road to wholeness requires a
healing of wounds, a binding up of broken relationships, a
return to a lost harmony. To wholeness and healing we can
add the word *holy*, which also belongs to that same family.
The life of prayer is the holy life seen as a movement of
healing and wholeness in the power and love of the Holy
Spirit.

Converse with God: God's Spirit and Our Spirit

In the Old Testament the Holy Spirit is called *ruach*, which
means "breath" or "wind" in Hebrew, and refers most often
to a powerful kind of wind that stirs things up. *Ruach* is also
used when discussing human beings. It is yet another way of
talking about our being made in God's image. Our *ruach* is
our likeness to God, our openness to him, and our possibil-

ity of communication with him. Genesis shows us the breath of God in bringing the cosmos out of chaos and ordering and garnishing everything that was made. The Spirit–Breath interacts with men and women. The Bible uses homely images to describe our intimacy, our interaction, with the Holy Spirit. Our converse with God is like a conversation with a friend in a garden, or a fierce argument, or an ominous scene in a courtroom. The Spirit of God accuses us, contradicts and confuses us, renders us obstinate. He also comforts, controls, fills, and inspires us. Both parties speak up to one another. Prayer is thus a free interchange: spirit to Spirit.

Another characteristic of the relationship between the Holy Spirit and our spirit is that God approaches the human situation with reference and takes risks as he commits himself into the power of those whom he chooses as his messengers. He entrusts his message to the prophets and leaves it to them to pass it on in their own words and to take the consequences for doing so. In the same way, the Spirit inspires the writers of Scripture, accepting their intellectual and cultural limitations and taking the risk of having his words misunderstood and misinterpreted. When we consider some of the actions ascribed to God in the more savage parts of the Old Testament and compare them with the Gospels, we have some sympathy with the remark of a child, "God does seem to improve as he gets older, doesn't he?"

God's action within Scripture is often a deeply hidden one, conveyed to us through layer upon layer of difficult material—the bloody rubble of the city of Jericho, or the stones of despair in the ruined city of Jerusalem. In other places whole tracts of material, filtered likewise through human experience, are luminous with mercy and loving kindness. God's action, in other words, covers the whole range of human experience. It is not always easy for us to see the work of God, the Holy Spirit, in human events or in the events described in the Bible. When we seek to understand the Word of God speaking to us through the Bible, we need the help of the same Spirit who inspired it. In this way we can sort out a superficial understanding from the abiding truth that lies under the surface. The Word of God is found in Scripture, but we have to dig for it. As the new Catechism puts it, we call the Holy Scriptures "the Word of God because God inspired their human authors and because God still speaks to us through the Bible."

Prayer Is the Holy Spirit Struggling within Us

There are many ways in which the Holy Spirit reveals the Father who sent him, reveals the Son to the world, and reveals us to ourselves. He is always opening things up to us in a marvelously self-effacing way. The Holy Spirit does not point to himself. Consequently, theology has had a hard time concentrating on him. God, the Holy Spirit, is always beyond us, on the move, creating and sustaining all things. The Holy Spirit is the *Go-Between God,* a God who works anonymously and on the inside, as *the beyond in our midst.*

There is so much one could say about the Holy Spirit. From the riches of tradition about the Holy Spirit, witnesses from Scripture, theology, worship, the history of the Church, and the lives of Christians, we have chosen three ways of looking at the work of the Spirit, particularly as they help us to understand our primary concern, which is the life of prayer. They are:

- the working of the Holy Spirit deep within the human spirit to judge, to confront, and to reconcile;
- the illuminating and sanctifying work of the Spirit;
- the creative work of the Spirit within the natural order and within the human community; the Spirit as the universal light.

The Action of the Spirit within Us: to Confront Us and Help Us Grow

According to the Gospel of St. Mark, after Jesus' baptism, "The Spirit immediately drove him out into the wilderness" (Mk. 1:12). Many of us find it difficult to believe that God is capable of tempting anyone, and this consideration has made it difficult for us to understand the phrase in the Lord's Prayer: "Lead us not into temptation." How can we believe that God would lead anyone into temptation? The new translation, "Save us from the time of trial," helps us to understand that in its original context the word *temptation* referred not to our small daily difficulties and humiliations, but rather to that universal and radical testing that was expected to come at the end of the world. It was a dreadful specter, a horrifying possibility. "And if the Lord had not shortened the days, no human being would be saved . . ." (Mk. 13:20a).

The testing that Jesus entered before he began his ministry is summed up for us in the three familiar scenes, those dialogues with Satan, which we find in Mark 1:12–13 (the Gospel appointed for the first Sunday in Lent, in Year B). God indeed did lead or drive his own Son, the Word made flesh, into the naked confrontation with evil itself. God is that tough. He also allows us to be tempted, to the limit of our power and even beyond. It is then that God provides a way through. Of course our temptations are puny compared with Jesus', but they are nevertheless as real and as necessary to us and to our growth and vocation as they were to Jesus. The Holy Spirit does lead us into situations in which we are tempted and that call us from an effort to sort out and to choose from various possibilities, and in the end to affirm the highest good. Our capacities are stretched beyond their limits, as God makes a way for us through the temptation, and we grow through the experience.

God, the Holy Spirit, comes to us in the most ordinary of circumstances. Imagine a morning when, at the Eucharist, the deacon spilled the contents of the chalice all over a small child. Although the child was embarrassed, she was soon reassured, cleaned up, and provided with a fresh blouse from the mission store. Thus equipped and encouraged, she was able to reenter the company of the worshiping community. The deacon was upset also, but she used the occasion to gain new insight into the meaning of her office— how it is to be carried out. She recognized her need to be quieter and more reflective as she administered the chalice and more aware of those who were receiving. "I miscalculated what the child could do." The deacon was also able to pull something beautiful out of a small incident that could have weakened and confused her rather than enlarging her view of things. Grace, the Go-Between God, the anonymous Holy Spirit—are they not pointing to the same divine activity, the activity of healing and reconciliation?

The Spirit Illuminates and Sanctifies

St. Paul speaks about the costly work of reconciliation that goes on in the midst of the whole creation. He describes us "who have the first fruits of the Spirit" as "groaning inwardly," waiting for adoption and redemption. We are exhorted in the Epistle to the Ephesians not to "grieve the Holy Spirit of God" (4:30). In the deep and painful struggle, often over trifles, which goes on within us, we confront the Spirit who can be grieved, and we receive fresh vision as to who we are and who is the God who has chosen us.

Just as the Holy Spirit struggles with us and shows us our sin for what it is, he also illuminates and sanctifies us. He enables us to have a free relationship with himself. He is the Spirit of wisdom who "searches everything, even the depths of God" (1 Cor. 2:10). He makes us understand more and more the gifts he has given us. He interprets spiritual truth for those who "possess the Spirit" (1 Cor. 2:12–13).

The Spirit Is the Creative Energy
behind All Things

The Spirit speaks to us through the created world in its wonder and beauty; it may be through natural beauty, like a mountain, a valley, the sea, a leaf, or a shell on the beach; it may be through the sudden impact of a painting in an ancient church; it may be through music, poetry, or someone's journal, or a thousand other things.

In the *Confessions* (Book IX, Ch. 10), St. Augustine

describes a little scene with his mother at Ostia, when "she and I stood alone, leaning at a certain window which overlooked the garden of the house we occupied in Ostia on the Tiber," discussing what the eternal life of the saints must be like. As they talked, they were carried upwards in their spirits, "through all bodily things," passing beyond their own minds' limits to the place where "life is that Wisdom by which all things are made . . . . And while we spoke and longed for that, we touched it for a moment with the whole effort of our heart . . . ."

The Holy Spirit quietly and unassumingly possessed them as they talked and took them beyond their own limitations. They caught a vision of life as it is held in being by the Spirit of God.

How does our understanding of the work of God, the Holy Spirit, affect our life? Think about the human spirit. It is given various names: mind, heart, soul. It is a word that covers all our energies as human beings and can be directed to bad as well as good ends. We are most ourselves when our spirit is open and receptive to God's Spirit.

Note

---

1. See also Ezekiel 37:5. Here, breath equals *spirit*.